Interviewing
for Success

ARTHUR H. BELL, PH.D.
DAYLE M. SMITH, PH.D.
School of Business and Management
University of San Francisco

NETEFFECT SERIES

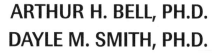

PEARSON
Prentice
Hall

Upper Saddle River, New Jersey
Columbus, Ohio

Vice President and Publisher: Jeffery W. Johnston
Senior Acquisitions Editor: Sande Johnson
Assistant Editor: Cecilia Johnson
Editorial Assistant: Erin Anderson
Production Editor: Holcomb Hathaway
Design Coordinator: Diane C. Lorenzo
Cover Designer: Jeff Vanik
Cover Image: Corbis
Production Manager: Pamela D. Bennett
Director of Marketing: Ann Castel Davis
Director of Advertising: Kevin Flanagan
Marketing Manager: Christina Quadhamer
Composition: Carlisle Communications, Ltd.
Printer/Binder: R.R. Donnelley & Sons Company
Cover Printer: Phoenix Color Corp.

Pearson Education Ltd.
Pearson Education Singapore Pte. Ltd.
Pearson Education Canada, Ltd.
Pearson Education—Japan

Pearson Education Australia Pty. Limited
Pearson Education North Asia Ltd.
Pearson Educación de Mexico, S.A. de C.V.
Pearson Education Malaysia Pte. Ltd.

10 9 8 7 6 5 4 3 2 1
ISBN 0-13-033530-4

Dedicated with love
to Chuck, Julie, Emily, and Megan Bell

Contents

3

4

5

6

Interview Testing 77

7

The Selection Interview, Performance Appraisal Interview, and Exit Interview 91

8

The Counseling Interview, Information Interview, and Negotiation Interview 105

Preface

Minute for minute, the most crucial time spent for business people is in interviews. For job seekers, the interview determines in large part who gets hired. For managers doing the interviewing, these occasions give the company a chance to add to its talent pool and increase its competitive advantage.

This book is a success guide for interviewers and interviewees who want to make the most of interview opportunities. Chapter 1, Getting to Know What Interviewers Do and Expect, takes the reader immediately to where the action is by looking over the shoulder of interviewers as they take on the various roles required for thorough interviewing, strategize for learning as much as possible about the job seeker, and evaluate the information they receive. Chapter 2, The New World of Structured Interviewing, reveals the newest approaches to behavior-based interviewing now being used by most Fortune 500 companies and many smaller firms. This chapter shows interviewers how and why to conduct a structured interview and teaches interviewees how to succeed in this new interview environment.

Chapter 3, Verbal Techniques for Interviewing, and Chapter 4, Nonverbal Techniques for Interviewing, focus on ways an interviewee can communicate most persuasively with an interviewer. Dos and don'ts are suggested and explained for verbal techniques involving tone of voice, volume, face, emphasis, pauses, articulation, and pitch. On the nonverbal side, guidance is given for effective eye contact, posture, gestures, facial expressions, and dress.

Chapter 5, What to Do When Interview Questions Turn Illegal, defines what interviewers can and can't ask—and shows interviewees what to do when interviewers' questions cross into illegal territory. Chapter 6, Interview Testing, describes the many forms of personality tests, skill tests, integrity tests, drug tests, and other evaluations that can accompany the interview. Chapters 7 through 10 discuss the various forms of interviews, with dozens of sample questions for the selection interview, performance appraisal interview, exit interview, counseling interview, information interview, negotiation interview, persuasion/sales interview, disciplinary interview, career-planning interview, focus group interview, and news/press conference interview. The book concludes with recommended reading for further information and guidance on the interview process.

Throughout, the most important points of these chapters are highlighted in "Insight" boxes, followed immediately by "Your Turn" opportunities for the reader to jot down reactions, reflections, experiences, and opinions. This interaction between authors and readers creates a conversation of sorts that leads to individualized strategies for successful interviewing. Both authors welcome contact at bell@usfca.edu.

ACKNOWLEDGMENTS

We are indebted to the scores of business researchers and scholars who have investigated and written about the interview process. We are also grateful to those at the front line of interviewing—the many executives and managers who have told us about their interview experiences, allowed us to observe their interview procedures, and involved us in evaluating their interview success. The list of these individuals over the years is long indeed, but we acknowledge here our special thanks to business leaders at Price-Waterhouse Coopers, PaineWebber, TRW, Lockheed Martin, Citicorp, Sun Microsystems, Charles Schwab, Genentech, American Stores, Cost Plus World Market, China Resources, Guangdong Enterprises, U. S. State Department, U. S. Coast Guard, Central Intelligence Agency, Colonial Williamsburg Foundation, New York Life Insurance, IBM, Pacific Bell, British Telecommunications, Deutsche Telekom, Cushman Wakefield, Star-Kist, and Quaker Oats.

Our sincere thanks to those individuals who reviewed this project in manuscript form and offered constructive feedback. They are Ashley Bishop, DeVry Institute of Technology; Barbara Limbach, Chadron State College; Cecilia Maldonado, University of Nevada, Las Vegas; and M. Duncan Rinehart, University of Colorado at Boulder.

We also thank our many supportive colleagues and friends at the University of Southern California, Georgetown University, the Naval Postgraduate School, the Thunderbird School of Management, the University of Arizona, and the University of San Francisco for their insights and influence: Professors Tom Housel, Bill Murray, Zhan Li, Les Myers, Steve Alter, Karl Boedecker, Barry Doyle, Mike Middleton, Steve Calvert, Joel Oberstone, Peggy Takahashi, Heather Cowan, Caren Siehl, Mary Ann von Glinow, Norman Sigband, Douglas McCabe, Denis Neilson, Steve Huxley, Alev Efendioglu, Heather Hudson, Roger Chen, Richard Puntillo, Diane Roberts, Eugene Muscat, Rex Bennett, Todd Sayre, Mark Cannice, Sheryl Barker, David Bowen, Cathy Fusco, Dan Blakley, Carol Graham, and Dean Gary Williams.

Getting to Know What Interviewers Do and Expect

GOALS

- Understand the various roles taken on by interviewers as a way of coming to know the interview process.

- Grasp the importance of interviews as key periods for decision making and opportunity.

- Begin to develop personal strategies for success as an interviewee and interviewer.

Most readers of this book have already been an interviewee at least once, perhaps for a job opportunity, an admission slot at college, or a place in a sorority, fraternity, sport team, club, or other organization. Some readers have also been interviewers on some of these occasions. Perhaps you have had to make the difficult decision whom to admit to an organization, whom to hire, or whom to lay off or terminate.

You probably remember vividly your activities as an interviewee and/or interviewer. Who can ever forget his or her first job interview? You no doubt sensed at the time how important these interview moments were not only for you but for others in the room with you. In the case of a hiring interview, the company had much to gain or lose in its choice among candidates. In the case of a college interview, what you said and how you presented yourself may have influenced where you attended college, what careers you prepared for, and where you ended up living and working.

This book is for people who recognize the importance of interviews and want to perform well in them, as both an interviewee and interviewer. Because the selection or hiring interview is the most common and most important interviewing experience for most readers, this book focuses primarily on that form of interviewing. But once hired, readers need to know about the other kinds of interviews treated in subsequent chapters: the performance appraisal interview, the exit interview, the counseling interview, the information interview, the negotiation interview, the persuasion/sales interview, the disciplinary interview, the career-planning interview, the focus group interview, and the news/press conference interview. These interview occasions can figure importantly in determining one's career success. It's vital to know what they are, how they work, and what you can do to participate in them professionally.

A quick scan through the pages of this book will reveal perhaps its most useful feature for those interested in interviewing: dozens upon dozens of actual interview questions you can use to practice your role as either an interviewee or interviewer. Although no one can tell you precisely what to say for any given question, we can offer advice on how to make your point effectively and strategically, including how and where to place emphasis to make your responses memorable and influential.

INSIGHT 1	*Knowing as much as possible about interview types and processes gives you the best chance to prepare for success in these professional situations.*

Your Turn	

Using a separate sheet, create a "T"-chart of two columns. In the first column, enter all positive memories and impressions you have of your last interview (or a particularly memorable interview). In the second column, enter all negative memories and impressions of the interview you have chosen. Using the space below, conclude this exercise by writing down what you could have done, if anything, to convert some of the negative characteristics into positives.

(lined writing space)

WHO IS YOUR INTERVIEWER?

One of the best ways to prepare for an interview is to understand the role of interviewers. Who are these people? What are they trying to do during the interview session? What do you need to know to understand "where they are coming from"?

The modern interviewer wears many hats and often changes them without notice to the interviewee. Reflect for a moment on the complex, shifting current of activities that takes place in even a short interview.

Establishing a Relationship

Often in half an hour or less the interviewer is expected to get a relationship off on the right foot—and not only a personal relationship ("Hi, George, I'm Alice Parker") but also a budding relationship between you (the candidate) and the company. That's a tall order for such a limited time span, especially when nerves are running high and the situation itself is somewhat stressful.

> _Interviewers build relationships with candidates as a way of gaining trust, opening channels of communication, and inviting candid opinions and disclosure._   **INSIGHT 2**

Your Turn

Write briefly about a time when an interviewer failed to establish what you considered to be a good relationship in your interview. How did the lack of that relationship affect your performance in the interview and the outcome of that interview?

Collecting Information

You come to the interview prepared to "dump" dozens of items of information on the interviewer—past jobs, past experiences, present abilities and attitudes, future aspirations, and so forth. Often these items come in rapid fire during conversation, with no particular order. The interviewer is expected to catch whatever you, the candidate, pitch—all the while maintaining rapport, asking questions, showing interest, and maintaining control of the interview. A court reporter would be challenged to collect all the information an interviewer is expected to gather. Diligent note taking may not be the answer for the interviewer if such activity interferes with eye contact and other signs of sincere interest.

Guiding Conversation

The interviewer comes to the interview with certain subjects she wants to cover. At the same time, you as the job candidate come to the interview with your own list of items you wish to talk about. Given these different agendas, one of the most difficult tasks for an interviewer therefore is keeping the interview on course and on schedule, with appropriate portions of time provided for the topics that matter most during the interview.

Probing

The interviewer wants the session with the candidate to provide more information and insight than a resume could. Therefore, the interviewer digs a bit here and there to clarify facts, uncover additional information, and invite disclosure on the part of the candidate. This process of probing isn't easy to master. The interviewer spends energy not only in thinking about ways to phrase probing questions but also in evaluating the emotional tone of those questions. Will a particular probe sound hostile, suspicious, or picky? Will the probe suggest that the interviewer hasn't heard or understood what the candidate has already said?

INSIGHT 3	*Interviewers probe not primarily because they suspect the candidate is hiding the truth. Instead, most probes are an effort to understand the candidate's points more fully.*

Your Turn

Think about the probes you use when you want to understand more completely what someone is trying to tell you. List those probes. Which could you use as an interviewer?

Interpreting Facts, Representations, and Feelings

In the microseconds of "free time" left between all these activities, the interviewer attempts to assemble an accurate picture of you, the candidate, from the many pieces of conversation flying by. What goes on inside an interviewer's mind can come to sound like a Ping-Pong game, with the candidate throwing more and more balls onto the table: "He worked with mainframe computers, but not micros. He supervised four people, all of them more experienced than he was. He's held four jobs in the past five years." Each item of information must be given a value of some sort that contributes to the interviewer's ultimate judgment of you. All the while, feelings and impressions are influencing how the interviewer evaluates you and vice versa.

Recording Information and Judgments

To add to all this complexity, the company has probably provided the interviewer with a score sheet or other note-taking page that is supposed to be filled out during the heat of the chase. These sheets can be complicated, asking the interviewer to fill out everything from the candidate's demeanor ("Confident?" "Friendly?") to graduation and employment dates. The stakes for thoroughness and accuracy are high for such note taking. Federal and state laws require observable and preservable data to support the interviewer's judgments, particularly when protected groups are involved, as defined by Title VII legislation and other law.

Giving Information

The interview is a two-way street. The interviewer and the company are being appraised by the candidate at the same time that the candidate is being evaluated for a job opening. During the interview, the interviewer not only must gather information but also must disperse it. Much of this information is predictable: benefit plans, current company projects, future prospects, and so forth. But the interviewer also has to be ready to field unexpected questions. "On average," you ask, "how many promotions are made from my job level to the next level each year?" If the interviewer equivocates ("I'm not sure, the number varies"), your interest in the job may flag. Part of an interviewer's preparation for your interview, therefore, is to assemble information for ready access.

INSIGHT 4	*Interviewers provide a two-way channel of communication. On the one hand, they try to gather information from the candidate. On the other hand, they try to communicate company information to the candidate.*

Your Turn

Recall a recent interview in which you were the interviewee. Estimate the amount of time the interviewer spent talking. Next, categorize such talking into its main topics (such as company information and job details). Did you feel that the interviewer did too much of the talking in your interview?

_____

_____

_____

_____

_____

Creating Impressions

The interviewer's face, dress, posture, words, and silences—all these and more create impressions for you, the candidate. At the same time, these same impression makers from the candidate are forging images and attitudes that influence the interviewer. Candidates are often surprised to learn that the actual words they said during the interview were less influential than their appearance, rapport, and energy in coming out on top in a job interview.

THE SIX HATS OF A SUCCESSFUL INTERVIEWER

It is to your advantage as a job candidate to know the various roles an interviewer plays—the "hats," as it were, that he wears during the interview. By recognizing which hat the interviewer wears at any given moment in the interview, you as a job candidate gain an important head start in grasping where the interviewer is headed in conversation and what he or she seeks from you.

Hat 1: The Detective

In virtually all types of interviews the interviewer will attempt to probe beneath surface answers in the search for truth. Like a detective, the interviewer is constantly involved in the activities of collecting and interpreting clues—a reservation here, an exaggeration there, a hesitation or show of temper. These are the materials by which the interviewer turns the raw data of your interview into a meaningful basis for decision making. Here's an example of the detective at work:

The Detective at Work

Q. You smiled when you mentioned your former boss. Anything you want to share?

A. (chuckles) He was a funny guy. He just couldn't stand competition. Had to have everyone under his thumb.

Q. You felt pushed around?

A. Well, I didn't feel that way because I wouldn't let him control me. But almost everyone else did.

Q. How did you react to his management style?

A. I just went around him.

Q. In what way?

A. (begins to clam up) Well, nothing in particular. Actually, we got along fairly well once I let him know my limits.

(The detective interviewer in this case makes a note to review the candidate's relations with past bosses.)

As a detective, the interviewer must keep up with both federal and state legislation guiding what can and can't be asked in interviews. In addition to knowing the law, the interviewer must be able to apply the law to questions, comments, probes, and procedures. All the while the interviewer must build a climate of trust with the candidate. Interviewees who sense that the interviewer is trying to trip them up will resort to game playing of their own: half-truths, overstatements, and defensive posturing.

> *Detective work on the part of the interviewer involves close attention to the details provided by the interviewee—and especially to the way those details fit together.* **INSIGHT 5**

Your Turn

Write about a time when an interviewer quizzed you in detail about certain aspects of your background or resume. How did you feel during this quiz? What could the interviewer have done to make his detective work as friendly as possible?

_____

_____

_____

_____

_____

Hat 2: The Merchant

Especially in hiring interviews, the interviewer is being sent by the company on an explicit buying trip. She is expected to examine the goods (you and your competitors for the position) and bring home the best of the lot. A manager's career, in fact, often rises or falls based on the soundness of hiring decisions.

The process of buying occurs in familiar stages. First, the buyer finds the right source of goods so as not to waste time. Second, he decides how to go about bargaining. If aloofness will bring price concessions on the part of the seller, the buyer must show a reserved manner. If on the other hand the buyer feels that charm will grease the wheels of the buying process, he pours his warm fuzzies. Third, he firms up the deal—precisely what he's getting and what he's paying are agreed upon.

Interviewers consciously or unconsciously employ that same buying process in hiring interviews. What adds interest to the process, of course, is that a double game is being played. From the interviewee's point of view, she is trying to "buy" a job by using the currency of education and experience. At the same time the interviewer is trying to "buy" the best candidate by using the inducements of salary and benefits.

The Merchant at Work

Q. As we discussed on the phone, this company is looking for a rare person—someone with computer expertise and strong word skills. Tell me about the lab manual you wrote as a teaching assistant.

A. Well, at State University our mainframe computing system had quite a few quirks that weren't covered in the factory manuals. I organized all these special cases into a supplemental manual that was published by the university. It's still being used there.

Q. Do you like to do such technical writing?

A. I do, probably because it comes easily to me. Once you understand an aspect of technology, it's satisfying to be able to explain it clearly to others.

Notice that the merchant interviewer is following the standard process of buying in this interview. The interviewer first states what the company is looking for, then begins squeezing the tomatoes, so to speak, in search of Mr. or Ms. Right.

Interviewees rightly feel that they must sell themselves and their abilities during an interview. But they often fail to realize that the interviewer is equally conscious of attracting and "buying" top talent for the company.   **INSIGHT 6**

Your Turn

If you have been interviewed by someone who obviously wanted you for the job at hand, what specific behaviors let you know that you were being courted for the position? If you have not had this experience, tell what an interviewer could do to let a candidate know how much the company wants to hire him or her.

_____

_____

_____

_____

_____

Hat 3: The Judge

In many interview situations, the interviewer sits as judge and jury over a candidate's professional future with the company. Rarely is there a route of appeal—the interviewer's verdict is final.

In such a high-stakes environment, the interviewer, no less than a court judge, must adhere to a firm sense of personal ethics and must beware of personal bias. The obvious biases—race, religion, age, gender—may be easier to exclude from the interviewing process than the subtle biases that too often let good candidates slip through a company's fingers (and sometimes into the courts for legal action!). Look at the following examples of such biases:

■ **The bothersome habit.**   She smacks her lips before speaking. He adjusts his tie every two minutes. For the careless interviewer, these personal habits become a mask that hides the real candidate. When impressions are distorted by such flak, the decision-making process breaks down. Interviewers are not so naive, of course, as to write down "smacks her lips" as a reason for rejecting a candidate. But they do err just as seriously when they invent reasons to cover their tracks—reasons that, when challenged in court, may prove quite expensive to the company.

■ **The nettlesome comment.**   Especially on stressful days, we each have "triggers" that can inadvertently be tripped. It can be a wholly innocent remark: **Q.** "Were you able to find parking?" **A.** "Yes, but I had to drive around for 20 minutes looking. Is it always this bad?" An overly sensitive interviewer could bristle at this remark, concluding that "this guy is a complainer." Accomplished interviewers resist drawing conclusions based on a single comment. They wait to see whether such comments form a trend in the person's expressions or behavior.

■ **The kiss of death.**   Sometimes the candidate comes to the interview trailing clouds of glory or gore. In either case, a good interviewer discounts what others say about the candidate. The kiss of death can come from one of the interviewer's colleagues—"I spoke briefly with that candidate. You won't be impressed." Just as often a comment can come from the interviewer's secretary: "I think you'll like Kay. She's very sweet." Perhaps the most insidious form of influence comes from friends and superiors. Like the rest of us, interviewers want social approval and the boss's blessing. It's difficult to ignore what friends and supervisors have to say, pro and con, about a job candidate.

■ **The objectionable look.**   Perhaps it's a particular style of dress or tie or accessories. Most interviewers will admit to a look of one kind or another that they just don't like. Often that look recalls for them someone from their past or from the movies. It takes considerable insight and self-control for an interviewer to see past the objectionable look to the talent of the candidate at hand. As a job candidate, you probably will not know in advance what styles of dress or grooming your interviewer likes or dislikes. The best rule of thumb, therefore, is to present yourself in a way that shows your respect for the company and the interview process.

The Judge at Work

Q. You've told me about your sales experiences. How do you feel about cold calling?

A. (hesitates) I've done some. It isn't particularly hard for me.

Q. You like it?

A. Well, no one likes cold calling. But it has to be done. I don't have a problem with it.

Q. (tests tentative judgment) I guess it's hard on the ego to be turned down by people you don't know.

A. It sure is. But, as I say, I can do it.

In this case, the interviewer arrives at an eventual judgment based in large part upon the hesitations and reticence of the interviewee.

We all occasionally err by making judgments too quickly about other people and their ideas.	**INSIGHT 7**

Your Turn

Write about a time when you made an early, incorrect judgment about a person, idea, or situation that later proved to be much more positive in nature than you had foreseen. What did you learn from this experience?

_____

_____

_____

_____

_____

_____

Hat 4: The Professor

Many selection interviews are primarily informational in nature. Candidates want to hear about the company—and the company wants to tell its story. In these situations, the interviewer plays the role of professor, with all the dangers traditionally associated with this profession. Professors carry the reputation of being boring and detached from "real life."

As an interview candidate, you may have to remind yourself to stay awake and appear interested when an interviewer lapses into any of the following three behaviors associated with professors:

■ **The lecture.**   An interview is supposed to be a two-way flow of conversation. Too often, an interviewer uses most of the interview time to deliver a lecture showing off his expertise but not investigating yours.

■ **The distraction.**   Some interviewers in the role of professor go off on tangents. Although you as the interviewee may not be able to control these detours, you can resolve to make your own key points in a succinct way, using phrases such as "Here's the bottom line for me ... here is what's most important in my opinion ... I think it all adds up to this. ... "

■ **Words, words, words.**   Interviewers in the role of professor forget that images have powerful communication value. They talk their way through the company history and projects instead of handing you, the candidate, an annual report or recent brochure to peruse. Don't make this mistake when your turn comes to put your best foot forward. Bring along a portfolio of materials that support your claim to expertise and excellence. Such materials can include reports, presentation pages, product or project data, commendations—anything that helps to make your case visually as well as verbally.

The Professor at Work

Q. Let me tell you a bit about the history of the company. It was founded in 1988 by Allen Dwight, an electrical engineer with a patent on a unique kind of computer router. Our first customers were military and academic clients. But the company really began to grow in the mid-1990s when we won a contract for an early form of a wireless network (notices a glaze settling over the candidate's eyes). Have you worked with wireless networks?

A. Uh, yes. My senior project involved an architecture for a wireless Intranet.

Q. Well, after that breakthrough for the company we became known as the industry leader for high-quality, reliable routers ... (and the lecture continues).

What is a candidate to do when the professor/interviewer talks on and on? Sometimes it's simply best to listen politely, because interviewers who like to hear themselves talk often give highest marks to candidates who seem to enjoy listening. But often it's important to make an impression and convey your opinions without appearing to interrupt the professor's endless lecture. You can do so by asking a question. In the example just given, the interviewee could have replied as follows to the interviewer:

> "Yes, my senior project involved an architecture for a wireless Intranet. Does your company target the Intranet market?"

That kind of question forces the professor/interviewer to relate what the company does to what you, the candidate, have to offer.

In interview situations, interviewees often have to act in their own best interests by regaining interview control from an interviewer who insists on doing most of the talking.

INSIGHT 8

Your Turn

Think about a time when you couldn't seem to get a word in edgewise with a person who talked, talked, talked. Write down strategies you used (or could use next time) for getting your own opinions expressed on such occasions.

_____

_____

_____

_____

_____

_____

Hat 5: The Priest

Especially in counseling interviews, the interviewer often plays the part of the priest (or minister, rabbi, etc.). He hears confessions of "sins," provides words of wisdom, and often closes the interview with guidance and encouragement (not unlike a blessing). The role of confidant can occur during selection interviews as well. Job candidates sometimes disclose quite personal information or feelings in the course of such interviews. In exit interviews, especially following layoffs or terminations, the door is open to the sharing of the full range of emotions, some of them raw and bitter.

When you are the interviewee in any of these circumstances, use caution in what you choose to disclose. The interviewer who takes on the role of the priest invites you to share thoughts and feelings without reservation—but you must be the one to determine how much or how little you should say. Watch especially for three intentional or unintentional pitfalls:

- **"It's off the record."** When a kind-faced interviewer says these words, you should make sure what he means. Will your answers and opinions be shared with others? If so, in what ways? What assurance do you have that the interviewer will keep his word?

- **"Let me share a secret with you."** The interviewer who breaks the confidence of others often does so in an effort to lure you into saying more than you want to about situations and personalities. Recognize that someone who breaks an agreement of confidentiality with someone else will probably do so with you as well.

- **"Here's what this means."** Interviewers sometimes overstep the boundary of their appropriate area and muck about as amateur psychiatrists. Don't be misled by an interviewer eager to draw conclusions about your personality, social relationships, or professional talents. The power that comes with the job of interviewing unfortunately corrupts some interviewers into self-appointed gurus. As an interviewee, you can object on the spot to the opinions of these would-be psychics or you can simply take their pronouncements with a grain of salt.

The Priest at Work

Q. You mentioned that you and Jack have problems working together. What's going on?

A. I just don't like his rough manner and his disorganized approach to management. Everything is always a panic with him.

Q. And that makes you angry?

A. (senses that the focus is shifting away from Jack's behavior) Yes, and I think I have good reason to be angry.

Q. Do you carry that anger home with you?

A. (at this point the interviewee sees that the interview is headed toward quite personal topics and therefore attempts to redirect conversation) I think we should talk about Jack's management style, not my home life.

Notice in this dialogue that the priest/interviewer strays into territory more appropriate for a therapist—not at all what the company intended. Interviewees who play into such conversation give away both their privacy and their power.

Human beings naturally disclose personal information as they grow to trust one another. In a professional context, exercise caution in making significant personal disclosures until you know well the person who invites such confidences.   **INSIGHT 9**

Your Turn

Relate the story of a time when you disclosed personal information to someone who later misused that information. What led you to believe you could trust the person? In what ways can you protect yourself against such abuse of personal information in the future?

_____

_____

_____

_____

Hat 6: The Salesperson

Finally, the company often sends interviewers into selection interviews as salespeople. In this role, the interviewer is supposed to guide the flow of conversation toward topics favorable to the company, including its culture, products, personnel, and policies. Selling, like courtship, must be more than a one-way activity. You, the job candidate, are an involved partner in the selling process—and it's up to you how involved you want to become. When you sense that the interviewer wears her salesperson hat, rely on your own good sense to watch for three sales ploys:

■ **"Tell the interviewee what he or she wants to hear."** As a job candidate, you probably have many questions about a potential employer: How and when do promotions occur? Is the company's financial future bright or cloudy? Will I be asked to relocate? In responding to these questions, an interviewer eager to "sell" you on a job opportunity may tell you what you want to hear rather than what's true. This is especially the case for companies that turn over hiring to interviewers who will have no further contact with candidates once they are employed. You can separate salesmanship from truthful disclosure by asking politely for examples or other support for an interviewer's assertions—and then using public information sources on the company to check for veracity. Let's say that your interviewer tells you "the company is doing great." You owe it to yourself to check that assertion against evidence you can find on the ups or downs of the company's stock, its earnings, and its rating by such sources at Standard & Poor's.

■ **"Emphasize the positive."**   If an interviewer insists on telling you only the bright side of work at the company, you should probe a bit into the rest of the story. You could ask, for example, "What challenges or obstacles does the company face in the short and long term?" By such questions you prevent an interviewer bent on salesmanship from leading you down a primrose path.

■ **"Trust me."**   A large part of the sales process is based on personal chemistry. The salesperson attempts to gain the client's trust so that the terms of the sale itself do not become an obstacle or issue. Some interviewers are adept at using this ploy with interviewees: "You won't be sorry you took this job—trust me." In fact, your evaluation of whether to take a particular job should not depend on your trust in an interviewer. Likewise, an ethical interviewer will not try to sway you solely on the basis of the trust factor.

The Salesperson at Work

Q.   Is there anything you would like to ask me about the company?

A.   Yes. What can you tell me about employee turnover?

Q.   We have our usual share, but the division you'll be working for is in good shape. You won't have a problem.

A.   Have there been layoffs recently?

Q.   We had a layoff a few months ago, but—trust me—you won't be affected by anything like that.

At this point the interviewee's internal alarms begin to sound. Little besides the interviewer's appeal to "trust me" assures the candidate that further layoffs are not imminent at the company.

INSIGHT 10	*Those who are understandably enthusiastic about a new position may be vulnerable to "sales" individuals who misuse that enthusiasm to control and persuade the candidate, often toward false ends.*

Your Turn

Write about a time you were "sold" on some item, idea, or experience—only to have buyer's remorse at a later time. Thinking back on that experience, what signs could have alerted you that you were under the influence of a "sales" person who may not have had your best interests at heart? What would you do differently the next time such a situation presents itself?

_____

_____

_____

_____

_____

_____

Knowing the hats that an interviewer wears can prepare you to interact effectively in the interview process. As in chess, success in the game of interviewing often requires the ability to foresee the other person's moves and strategies. A job candidate who recognizes in advance where an interview is headed has the best chance of participating in it advantageously.

Summing Up

Interviewers are not simply professional men and women who ask questions and listen to answers. Instead, they play out a series of complicated roles in their efforts to invite disclosure from candidates, probe for deeper meaning, and communicate messages about their companies. By understanding the motives and actions of interviewers, interviewees have the best chance to interact successfully and strategically with these individuals.

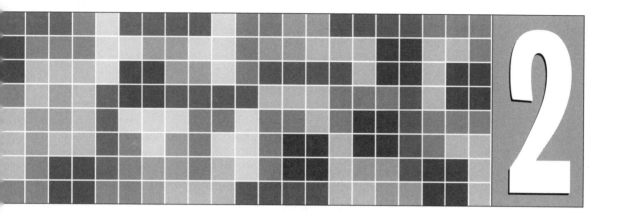

The New World of Structured Interviewing

GOALS

- Recognize that most large companies are now employing the techniques and methods of behavior-based structured interviewing.

- Understand why that approach to interviewing offers both the company and the interviewee the best chance for achieving a good hire.

- Review the biases that often creep into the interviewing process in the absence of interview rules and structures.

Your interviews to date may have been "old-fashioned" in the sense that no plan or structure determined what questions would be asked. The interviewer just seemed to chat with you about whatever came to his mind. Other applicants may have had quite different questions from the interviewer. In some cases, the interviewer may have done most of the talking.

That approach to interviewing is dying out. The great majority of Fortune 500 companies and government agencies are now beginning to use a relatively new interviewing technique called *behavior-based structured interviewing* (BSI). The success and legal advantages of BSI make it highly likely that you will encounter this new form of interviewing in the near future.

We don't want to give the impression that all companies now use the new form of interviewing described in this chapter. Many smaller firms continue to use more informal approaches to interviewing, in which an interviewer comes up with questions somewhat spontaneously. Some interviewers feel this traditional approach to interviewing provides an opportunity to establish person-to-person rapport, to get to know a job seeker in more depth, and to attain a better "feel" for how the candidate may fit into the company's workforce. The counterargument, as explained in this chapter, is that spontaneous interviews treat candidates unequally (by giving them different questions) and hence unfairly. As a job seeker, you will have little influence over what kind of interview a company decides to give you. But as an interviewer, you may have significant input in how your company designs its selection process. This chapter urges you to consider the many legal and strategic advantages of the structured approach to hiring.

INSIGHT 11	*The ways in which you were interviewed for jobs in the past may have changed substantially in recent years. Preparing for behavior-based structured interviews may mean un-learning some of the techniques you used for traditional interviews.*

Your Turn

Write about a time when you were interviewed in an unstructured manner. How did you feel about the interview experience? If others were also interviewed, what was their experience? Looking back on the interview, how do you think the interviewer decided whom to hire?

_____

_____

_____

_____

_____

_____

WHAT'S WRONG WITH OLD-STYLE INTERVIEWING?

"Our interviewers like the old-fashioned, seat-of-the-pants approach to hiring," one northern California real estate developer tells us. "It makes the interview more lively. You never know what you'll end up discussing with an applicant." She points out that experienced interviewers like to trust their intuitions—their "gut feelings"—to come up with the right questions and pick the right candidate. "And," concludes this executive, "it's an impossible task to plan what should be asked in all the various positions in the company. We have to trust our interviewers to ask the right questions."

This set of ideas is the general defense for old-fashioned interviewing. In addition to the arguments made by this developer, old-style interviewing has the weight of history on its side—it's "the way we've always done it"—and, in fact, it's the way most of us were interviewed for our present jobs.

But put yourself in the place of a job applicant. You are one among several candidates to be interviewed. Does it matter that the big boss in the office interviewed your competition, but you are to be interviewed by a lower-ranking manager? That the previous interviewee was taken out to lunch and you're "next up" at 2 P.M. in a cramped office meeting room? Of course it does. In traditional interviewing, the judgments of individual interviewers (and their relative clout in the company) can vary widely. If you're lucky, you will get an interviewer who likes you and has the status to help you get the job. The operative word is "lucky," not "fair" or "rational."

Traditional interviewing procedures offer little more than a random chance that winners will be chosen over losers, all because the many variables influencing the interview are not identified and managed.   **INSIGHT 12**

Your Turn

Write about a time when you felt that someone else had the "edge" or "best chance" for an opportunity of some kind. How could the interviewing process have been changed on that occasion so that all candidates had a fair chance to explain their abilities?

_____

_____

_____

_____

But play out the scenario. The interviewer begins his questions. Where do these questions come from, you wonder. Sometimes the interviewer glances at your resume as a stimulus for a question or two. Sometimes he stares at the ceiling, as if stuck for the next question. Often he asks you to repeat yourself. He doesn't take any notes.

Note that in this old-style interview, questions come "out of the blue," according to the whim of the interviewer. They are not formulated in advance in close coordination with job requirements. At best, they are conjured up by the interviewer in an attempt to "get an overall impression of the applicant" or to "see how the applicant relates and communicates" or "to keep things flowing." At worst, these questions are time wasters for both the company and the applicant—just "talk" that yields little valuable information about the candidate's suitability for the position. Freed from any interview plan, the typical old-style interviewer does up to 80 percent of the talking during the interview.

After 30 minutes, the interviewer rises and you shake hands. It's over. But you can't help noticing that the previous interviewee's session, with a different manager, ran much longer than yours. You suppose that it all depends on which interviewer an applicant happens to get—the luck of the draw. You have good reason for concern about the length of interviews; recent research demonstrates that successful candidates invariably are granted longer interviews than unsuccessful candidates.

As you leave the office, you wonder what's going to happen to the answers you gave to the interviewer. Will they be recorded or noted in any way? Will they be conveyed accurately to other decision makers in the company? Or will it all come down to the interviewer's gut feeling, a crude thumbs-up or thumbs-down based on personal impressions and vague criteria such as "the kind of person we're looking for" and "someone who will be a good fit"?

As you reflect on this interview experience, you feel you've just participated in a lottery of sorts. Your interviewer, the interview site, the length of the interview, the interview questions, and the recording and evaluation of your answers were all a matter of luck, not plan. No wonder that traditional interviewing so often produces the "halo effect," in which an interviewer simply hires the person who seems to be wearing a halo similar to the interviewer's. And, given the freedom to make up questions and to evaluate candidate responses as she wishes, no wonder the prejudices of an interviewer play such a major role in hiring. You can easily imagine an interviewer who consistently blocks the hiring path for women, or middle-aged men, or overweight applicants, or nonathletic types, or whatever other bias the interviewer applies in the hiring process. The door is wide open to prejudice, and no one is watching. There's also the danger of the cloning effect, in which an interviewer in effect hires candidates in his own image over and over for the company.

Powerful prejudices keep many people out of serious consideration for job opportunities because of their age, gender, ethnicity, or other factor.   **INSIGHT 13**

Your Turn

Think about people in your family or close group of friends. Write down the barriers some of these individuals would probably face if they were now interviewing for professional positions. Discuss how the interview system could be changed to give these individuals a fair chance for employment.

_____

_____

_____

_____

_____

_____

_____

The Legal Basis for Structured Interviewing

To all such matters of chance, gut feeling, and potential bias, the law related to hiring says "Stop!" Specifically, the Uniform Guidelines arising out of Title VII and Equal Employment Opportunity legislation insist that the interview be designed on the basis of specific job requirements. Both the content and the method of the interview must be developed to reveal accurately and fairly which candidates are best qualified to fulfill the job requirements determined by the company. If challenged in court, employers must be able to show that interview questions are directly related to these job requirements. In addition, employers must afford each candidate equal treatment in the screening process.

Allowing prejudice to exclude certain people from employment consideration is illegal and unethical.   **INSIGHT 14**

Have you or anyone you know been excluded from serious consideration for an employment or membership opportunity because of such factors as age, race, religion, disability, marital status, or economic status? If so, tell the story in detail. If not, discuss what you believe the courts can do to ensure fairness in hiring procedures.

_____

_____

_____

_____

_____

_____

Where Structured Interview Questions Come From

Since you are or soon will be on the receiving end of interview questions, you may well wonder where they come from. In creating interview questions, managers should look to those who know the job best: those who perform it successfully or supervise its performance in the company. These "hands-on" experts list "critical incidents" involved in the successful performance of the job. (A critical incident is a specific problem or challenge presented by the job together with a description of the behavior that solved the problem or met the challenge.)

The following example gives one critical incident from the analysis of an environmental specialist position.

Problem: Community groups have raised charges about potential environmental damage from a project development plan. They have the ear of city and county planning officials. How can the job candidate work effectively with such groups to achieve mutually acceptable goals?

Successful behavior: The candidate works patiently in a non-confrontational way to understand community concerns; remains highly visible as a company spokesperson; interacts well with city and county planners to further company goals; and works to focus community concerns on specific issues that the company can address successfully and economically.

This incident, drawn from actual work life and the job description for an environmental specialist, is one piece in the process of constructing job-based questions for use in interviews. If an employer knows what behaviors it takes to succeed in a given job, she can then develop interview questions and tests to locate people qualified to perform those behaviors. For some secretarial or reception positions, of course, the job analysis may involve only a handful of critical incidents. For more complex positions, the number of critical incidents may rise to a dozen or more.

These critical incident descriptions, once gathered, form the basis for "what it takes" to perform a particular job. By pinpointing the things that actually matter most, the employer has gone far to remove the element of guesswork from the hiring process.

Job descriptions arise out of a list of critical incidents specified by those who do the job best.

INSIGHT 15

Your Turn

Write down two critical incidents (two work behaviors that matter most for success) drawn from a job you now have or one from the past.

_____

_____

_____

_____

_____

_____

Developing the Job Analysis and Description

A job analysis team—perhaps only two or three people in a small office—usually comprises a manager deeply familiar with the job and one or more people who are good at the job. The team meets to organize the many critical incident descriptions into a succinct description of job behaviors—the "job description." The panel also considers the following:

- *Information sources of particular importance for the job.* Must the applicant, for example, be thoroughly familiar with a certain set of state or federal regulations? A particular database system?

- *Abilities in decision making or information processing critical to job performance.* Must the applicant be able to perform some mathematical operations in his head? Hold several numbers in mind at once? Review numbers quickly for accuracy?
- *Physical requirements, including coordination, stress, and dexterity.* Must the applicant be able to sustain periods of prolonged work stress during "crunch" times in the office or in public hearings? Sit at the computer or other office machines for hours at a time without physical problems?
- *Social skills required for the job.* Will the job entail the tactful supervision of others? Meeting clients and community groups in high-stakes, stressful contexts? Relating to coworkers as a motivational manager?
- *Scheduling and travel requirements of the job.* Must the applicant be ready to make scheduling changes and travel plans on short notice? Is the candidate available for overtime?

These types of items form the complete job description, only a summary of which will probably appear in journal, newspaper, or Internet "help wanted" ads for the position. "But all this might take hours!" comes the predictable complaint. Right—and those hours are a wise investment of time when compared with the months and years, perhaps, that the company may have to suffer with the wrong hire, all due to ill-considered interviewing techniques.

INSIGHT 16	*Job descriptions that do not depend on critical incidents are mere fictions— guesses by those who don't know what behaviors will lead to success or failure in the job.*

Your Turn

Write a brief job description for a job you now hold or have held in the past. Next, discuss the degree to which your job description is based on your knowledge of critical incidents related to that job.

_____

_____

_____

_____

Turning the Job Analysis into Interview Questions

With the completed job description before it, the team begins to formulate interview questions. These should be drawn from several types of questions to provide variety and to measure an interviewee's ability to respond to different forms of questions, including the following:

Definitional questions.   These are usually posed in a "What is a . . . " or "What does _____ refer to or mean?" format. They require applicants to demonstrate their knowledge of terms, concepts, and tools.

Causal questions.   These are posed in the format of "What happens when . . ." or "What is the result of . . ." Causal questions ask an applicant to specify the consequence of some initial act or procedure.

Hypothetical questions.   These questions take the form of "What would you do if . . ." or "What could happen if . . ." Hypothetical questions test the candidate's ability to handle future situations based on past learning and experience.

Situational questions.   Related in some ways to hypothetical questions, situational questions ask the applicant to put himself into a realistic circumstance described in detail by the interviewer. These questions usually take the form of "Here's the situation . . . What would you do?"

Simulational questions.   In these questions, the circumstance or situation is not described verbally to the applicant. Instead, the applicant is physically presented with some aspects of the job situation. Typically, simulation questions take the form of "To achieve the purpose of _____, you are now holding _____. Show what you would do to achieve your purpose."

Relational questions.   These ask the applicant to tell, perhaps by role playing, how she would handle interpersonal situations.

Explanatory questions.   These usually take the format of "Why would you . . ." or "How would you explain . . ."

Once questions and their answers have been selected according to the relative importance of job behaviors, the team must arrange them for *uniform* delivery to job applicants. Questions are often arranged to follow the course of a typical workday or the work cycle from the beginning to the end of production. Or, questions can be arranged in order of increasing or decreasing importance. In most cases, applicants will respond to questions more clearly and completely if the questions occur in a meaningful arrangement.

Good interview questions arise directly from the job description, which in turn is based on critical incidents.   **INSIGHT 17**

Your Turn

Pretend that you are preparing to interview a person for a job in a company at which you are now employed or in another organization. Use the questions types described previously to write at least five questions you would use in this imagined interview.

_____

_____

_____

_____

_____

_____

Training Good Interviewers

Employment managers often find that getting honest information from applicants is not nearly so big a problem as getting their interviewers to ask the questions set forth in the interview plan.

Interviewers, after all, are human beings with feelings for those they interview. Some job interviewers are reluctant to ask "hard" questions, particularly of applicants for whom they have an initial liking. Often in an effort to "help out" a congenial applicant, an interviewer may glide over such thorny areas as past firings, a succession of short job stays, or poor college performance. This quite human tendency on the part of the interviewer leaves an information gap for the company in its hiring process. The practice also discriminates against other applicants who, for whatever reason, aren't given special help from the interviewer.

These circumstances apply especially to situations in which only a few candidates may apply for a given job opening. "Shouldn't we make the interview kind of fun and enticing—you know, woo the right candidate?" some will suggest. There's nothing wrong with talking about all the good things your company has to offer. But managers should not compromise the fairness and objectivity of the interview process itself in a wrong-headed effort to charm certain candidates. They are risking legal entanglement and, more often, the possibility of a bad hire.

To keep the interview process fair and objective, all questions developed for a structured interview are asked in order and verbatim for each applicant. In structured interviewing, the interviewer can repeat a question if necessary, but cannot coach the applicant, give hints regarding the intent of or possible answers for the question, or otherwise influence the applicant's response. Also, the interviewer cannot indicate by verbal or nonverbal signals the relative success or failure of the candidate's answer. Saying "that's a great answer" or "you certainly know your field" to one candidate and not to another obviously gives one candidate an advantage.

Interviewers trained in structured techniques may seem less spontaneous and friendly than traditional interviewers. To be fair to all candidates, structured interviewers endeavor to give approximately the same interview opportunity to each applicant. **INSIGHT 18**

Your Turn

If you have experienced a structured interview, tell how you felt about the process. If you have not experienced this kind of interview, do you believe you could perform well under its rules and guidelines? Explain your response.

_____

_____

_____

_____

_____

_____

Scoring the Structured Interview

Unlike traditional interview results, structured interviewing offers a planned scoring system for each question used in the interview. At the time questions are developed for the interview, the team (as described earlier) works out a rating scale for a continuum of possible answers, ranging from a great answer to a poor one. Such judgments as "excellent" and "poor" are tied directly to behavioral objectives in the job analysis, not to the flair or style with which the candidate can schmooze. An excellent answer is one that reflects probable success in performing the related job task. A marginal answer is one that reflects probable difficulty in performing the job task. A poor answer is one that reflects probable failure in performing the related job task.

But who is to say which answers are excellent, marginal, or poor? That judgment is up to the same team members who know the job best and are familiar with employees' relative success in accomplishing it. In most cases, rating scales for interview questions are developed in brainstorming sessions by the job team. Excellent, marginal, and poor responses are specified as "anchors" on a five-point scale. Even though applicants may not hit any of these predicted answers on the nose, their responses can nonetheless be placed meaningfully at some point on the continuum marked by these anchors.

The following is an example from the title industry of an interview question and an accompanying rating scale. Note that these are not multiple-choice questions. Only the interviewers see the suggested responses following the question.

Question: "When reviewing a title search for a particular property, you come across a reference in a recorded document to 'other unrecorded covenants' related to a subject property. What do you do in reporting on the condition of title?"

5 (excellent)	Try to discover the nature of these unrecorded covenants and report the reference you found to your title officer.
3 (marginal)	Ask someone in the title office what to do.
1 (poor)	Ignore the reference entirely because it refers to unrecorded title information.

As an interviewee, you'll be glad to know that you aren't expected to say the precise words suggested in the anchor responses. Interviewers simply use these benchmarks to determine the appropriate numeric score of the applicant's actual answer. One or more interviewers mark scores for each question and also take notes on the content of the applicant's answer. After all applicants have been interviewed, the job team or other authorized hiring managers in the company begin the task of comparing, compiling, and reconciling their scores for individual applicants. If scores between raters differ by more than one number (for example, a "5" and a "3"), the team discusses the applicant's response and seeks to bring the scores closer together. Ratings are then averaged for each question and totaled as a record of the applicant's performance.

This scoring system makes it relatively easy to compare several candidates on the merit of their responses. It goes a long way toward eliminating distortions caused by interviewer bias, differences in questions, and such interpersonal factors as physical attractiveness, age factors, and style of dress.

INSIGHT 19	*A predeveloped scorecard for desired responses from interviewees gives interviewers the opportunity to discuss and settle upon the attributes and abilities they seek in a new employee.*

Your Turn

In what ways does structured interviewing level the playing field among job candidates from different cultural and socioeconomic backgrounds?

_____

_____

_____

_____

_____

Documenting the Structured Interview

Hiring managers have good reason to protect themselves against potential charges of discrimination in hiring. Most plaintiffs to date are successful in such suits, and court awards regularly run into the hundreds of thousands of dollars, especially when legal fees are included.

If a hiring discrimination suit is brought against a company, the court will insist on knowing the following information. These items are "must-haves" for documentation of the interview process:

1. _Document the job analysis process._ How is the job defined? How did the company determine the specific behaviors necessary for performing the job successfully?

2. _Document the process by which questions were created._ Who participated in their creation? Why were these people deemed competent to create the questions? How does each question asked in the interview relate to a behavior necessary for performing the job? In what ways do the number, type, and arrangement of questions reflect the proportionate importance of particular behaviors necessary to perform the job?

3. _Document the system by which applicant responses were scored._ What is the system? Who created anchoring responses? How do these anchoring responses relate to real levels of success among those actually performing the job? How were raw scores handled statistically? What weighting, if any, was used in the analysis of scores?

4. _Document the process of interviewing candidates._ How did applicants find out about the job? What were the criteria for choosing those applicants who were invited for interviews? Where and when were interviews conducted? Who served as interviewers? What are their qualifications, especially in relation to the job at hand? How were

questions delivered? How were responses noted? How long did interviews last? How did different interviews compare in time, content of questions, and method of evaluation?

5. *Document applicant responses and scores.* Notes taken by interviewers must be easily interpretable in reconstructing the approximate content of an applicant's response.

6. *Document the specific process by which one applicant was chosen over others.* What factors were involved? What was the weighting of those factors?

7. *Document the validity of the interview process.* Does the process in fact predict job performance?

This kind of documentation may seem burdensome to managers in some industries, but you can understand its necessity and importance. After all, the "due diligence" the court seeks in hiring matters is in line with more general social efforts to level the playing field for all job applicants, no matter what their age, gender, religion, ethnicity, or other personal factor.

INSIGHT 20	*Courts require companies to keep detailed records showing their hiring process and the ways in which that process was applied to hire candidates. Companies need to retain and interpret these records to make sure their interview procedures are producing the kind of new hires the company wants.*

Your Turn

Think about a selection procedure in which you were involved as an interviewer or decision maker. What kind of records did you keep? Would you recommend your approach to record keeping to companies and other professional organizations? Explain your answer.

_____

_____

_____

_____

_____

Certainly the work involved in "doing interviewing right" compares favorably, when facing suit, to the more dangerous course of trying to construct or fabricate a legally defensible hiring procedure after the fact. And why do disappointed job applicants sue? You name it: allegations of age discrimination, bias against ethnicity, preference for one gender over the other, violations of the Americans with Disabilities Act, and so forth. A small company is no less vulnerable than a large corporation as the target of such suits.

Examples of Behavior-Based Interview Questions

What an applicant has *done* is a better indicator of future job success than what the applicant believes, feels, thinks, or knows. The following questions are useful in getting applicants to discuss work realities rather than notions or suppositions. As a future job applicant, you can prepare for structured interviews by thinking through your responses to these questions.

Tell me how you increased teamwork among a previous group with whom you worked.

Describe what you liked and disliked about how you were managed in previous positions.

Recall a time when you made what you consider a mistake or a bad decision on the job. How did you handle the situation?

In your past work life, what kind of coworkers or clients rubbed you the wrong way? How did you respond?

Tell me about a time when you set specific work goals for yourself. How did things turn out?

Describe a time when you had to criticize or discipline the performance of someone who worked with you or for you. How did you handle the situation? What was the result?

Walk me through the major highlights of your career so far and tell me where you want to go next.

Tell me about a work emergency or crisis of some kind in which you were involved. What was your role? What did you do?

We've all felt stress in our work lives. Tell me about work-related situations that cause stress for you. How do you typically handle such stress?

In your most recent position, what did you learn? How did you apply this learning?

Tell me about a challenge you faced in a previous work situation. How did you respond?

Every manager has to learn to delegate well. Describe a work situation in which you delegated responsibility successfully. Next, tell me about a time when your delegation of responsibility did not work out well. How did you handle that situation?

What approaches worked best for you in the past in communicating with your boss? With your coworkers? With your subordinates?

Tell me about a time when you took charge as a leader in a work situation without being formally assigned to that role by your boss.

What experiences have you had working with people of different ethnicities, age, or physical ability levels?

In the past have you had a preference for working mainly with men or women? Explain your answer.

Tell me about a time when you felt you went beyond the call of duty in helping a client.

INSIGHT 21	A behavior-based question focuses on what the candidate has or can do, not on what the candidate thinks or feels.

Your Turn

Would you prefer to be hired based on your proven abilities or your ideas, aspirations, and philosophies? Explain your response.

_____

_____

_____

_____

_____

Useful Probes for Interviewing

Although probing for more extensive answers from candidates is not allowed in strictly structured interviewing environments, the practice is still widely used. It can be applied fairly if each candidate is given the advantage of approximately the same degree of probing by interviewers.

Please clarify what you mean by _____.

How did you feel when that happened?

Why do you think you reacted as you did?

Did you consider other options at the time?

Please give me more details about _____.

How do you think others felt about your actions at the time?

Looking back on the experience, how do you see things now?

What was going through your mind when you took that action?

Did the outcome of your action satisfy you?

Probes are used to help the interviewer and interviewee get to a fuller version of the truth.

INSIGHT 22

Your Turn

Discuss ways in which probes can be used without making the person being questioned feel attacked, doubted, or disrespected.

_____

_____

_____

_____

_____

Summing Up

For legal and financial reasons, the movement is definitely on toward behavior-based structured interviewing (BSI) in progressive American companies. Hiring managers have to be able to defend their hiring decisions in court, if necessary. That defense becomes almost impossible if hiring criteria, methods, and records have been handled in an unplanned and disorganized way. At the same time, companies want to improve the quality and efficiency of their hiring efforts. A structured hiring process can be evaluated and improved through repeated testing of its components. An unstructured process, by contrast, changes according to the whims of the interviewers.

BSI offers companies their best chance for bringing true performers into the company. At the same time, this approach to interviewing offers you, the job candidate, the best chance of being treated and evaluated fairly throughout the hiring process.

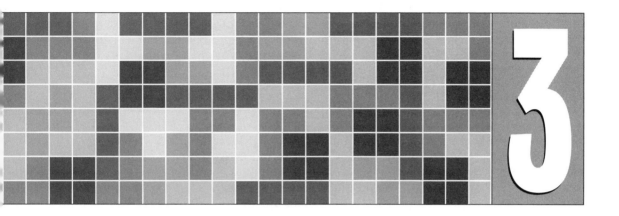

Verbal Techniques for Interviewing

COALS

- Identify primary verbal factors that contribute to interviewing success.
- Understand the challenges involved in changing personal habits having to do with verbal techniques.
- Master new approaches to verbal skills useful in expressing points clearly, persuasively, and memorably in interviews.

This chapter reminds you of the importance not only of what you say but how you say it—your tone, volume, pace, emphasis, pauses, articulation, pitch, and other verbal qualities. As you understand how to use these techniques to your advantage, you will also come to see how your interviewer uses verbal techniques as well to create impressions, motivate responses, and probe for additional information.

The content of your interview responses does matter, of course. But too many job seekers think that coming up with the "right" answer to an interview question will translate directly into interview success, in the same way that correct answers led to a high grade on a college exam. Nothing could be further from the truth. A job interview is not a school test. Instead, the interview provides a company with the chance to observe your professionalism, estimate your potential for successful interaction with clients and coworkers, and determine how well you present yourself and your ideas. These matters have relatively little to do with the "right" answer and everything to do with your verbal and nonverbal communication skills.

"I got the clear impression that he didn't like me," said Virginia R. as she left an interview for an accounting position with a southern California aerospace company. "It wasn't so much what he said as the way he said it."

The interviewer, Frank E., tells the other side of the story: "She was bright and had good background skills on paper, but she seemed timid and distant. I didn't think she would fit in with our accounting group."

In the fast Ping-Pong game of questions and answers in interviews, it's difficult to say who makes the first bad serve. But one thing's for sure: Once the ball begins to spin out of control, both players are put off their game.

INSIGHT 23	*Without well-developed verbal abilities, an interviewee cannot convey his excellence in other areas important for employment.*

Your Turn

Assess your own verbal abilities. Where do you feel you are particularly strong? What aspects of your verbal abilities need development?

_____

_____

_____

_____

_____

_____

_____

_____

_____

_____

_____

The ways in which words are said can drastically affect perceptions and actions. Call it the "restaurant effect." We've all been there: A waiter asks what we want to eat, but in the tone, volume, and pace we hear another message—"I'm tired and busy, Mac. Give me your order and be quick about it." That false start can influence how we feel about the food we eventually receive and about the restaurant itself. (A Boston communications firm, incidentally, does training workshops for waiters who want to improve their tips. The emphasis in these sessions, not surprisingly, is on tone of voice and personal manner.)

THE COMPONENTS OF VERBAL ACTION

Some interviewees think of the interview as a chance to convey content—facts, opinions, perspectives, anecdotes, achievements, and so forth. They rarely think about the verbal qualities of the interview, except to worry perhaps that nerves don't produce a quaver in the voice. Such interviewees need to understand that much of the real "action" in the interview isn't a matter of content at all. Action in the truest sense ("change of position or status under the influence of force") takes place on the verbal level as well as the content level. Your words and the way you say them are the primary movers and pushers in an interview, for better or worse. As suggested in the following figure, a verbal arsenal can be divided into seven categories, in order from the approximate greatest influencer to the least influencer:

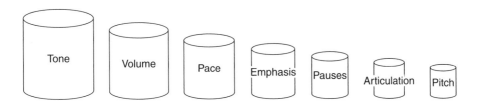

| **INSIGHT 24** | *What you say—and how you say it—in an interview is a form of action, just as surely as if you had jumped up and down physically.* |

Your Turn

Think for a moment about the idea that your way of saying things is a form of action expressed toward other people. In what ways can you make such verbal actions more effective? Discuss an actual situation or create a scenario to make your point.

Tone

By the time we're two years old we know how to recognize and interpret the tone of communication addressed to us: "Not now, Billy!" means Mom or Dad is close to anger. "Maybe in a little while," said in a surrendering tone, means we're closer to getting our wishes. By the time we're three or four, we've mastered the art of tone ourselves. We have learned to specialize in the pout, the taunt, the innocent alibi, the ultimatum, and all the other ways in which words are set apart by tone to mean something in addition to their dictionary meanings.

The art of tone is progressively refined as we mature. By the time we have entered our professional lives, we can shade our words with implied threat, suggested guilt, humor, sarcasm, intimacy, despair, and a wide range of other feelings and intentions. Above all, we have mastered by this time the "inner-outer" game in the tone we use. On the one hand, we choose a tone that tells something about how we feel on the inside about the words we're saying. When we reveal those feelings through our tone and other means, the listener feels that we're sincere—that is, our feelings square with the content of the words we're saying and actions we're taking.

On the other hand, however, we can choose a tone that is directed outward, not inward, to accomplish a particular purpose. This tone may or may not reveal our sincere feelings; its real intent is to produce certain responses within the listener. We choose an angry tone, perhaps, not because we're truly angry, but because we want the listener to think we're angry. We choose a tough, brusque tone in negotiations as a way of seeing what concessions the other party is willing to make.

Our tone is manipulative when it differs from what we, in fact, feel. Skilled interviewees and interviewers use both sincerity and manipulation in tone in their efforts to express themselves and influence the course of an interview.

Time out.   Is it ethical to "fake" feelings in your tone of voice to produce certain responses or reactions on the part of the interviewer? On this point we each make up our individual minds. Although the guiding principle to "be true to thyself" serves us well, we have all experimented at one time or another with a tone of voice that does not reflect fully or accurately how we feel. No matter what we individually choose to do with regard to the sincerity of our tone of voice, we can surely expect others—interviewers, for example—to take license in drawing on a wide range of verbal techniques, sincere and otherwise, in the course of the interview. (The most notorious example of such verbal techniques, perhaps, is the stress interview, in which the interviewer consciously tries to create a state of insecurity and disapproval in the interviewee. Does the interviewer mean all that she says? Probably not. It's a game, a technique, chosen to test the candidate.)

What a person "really means" or intends in an interview is often difficult to know. What a person says, however, is the stimulus that moves conversation along. Whether sincere or not, words once said have an action effect on all parties to the conversation.	**INSIGHT 25**

Your Turn

Have you ever played "devil's advocate" by expressing an opinion that you did not, in fact, hold sincerely as your own belief? In what ways can the technique of devil's advocate be useful for a full understanding of issues?

_____

_____

_____

_____

Varieties of Tone

Like personality itself, tone can take on many shadings and characteristics. When conversing with an interviewer, interviewees typically rely on four tone patterns in addition to the straight-forward tone used for most discussion:

The inquiring tone.   "You mentioned that the company had avoided layoffs to date. Do you think layoffs will be coming in the near future?" How does the interviewer respond when asked to substantiate or extend upon a point? For that matter, how do you respond as an interviewee when the interviewer calls into question one of your assertions? Laid on in an accusing way, this tone can produce indignation and a breakdown in communication. But used with discretion, the inquiring tone can serve as a useful scalpel in cutting through surface assertions to get at the real meaning beneath.

SAMPLE QUESTIONS USING THE INQUIRING TONE

- What real supervisory duties would I be performing in my first six months?
- As you think about promotions during the last six months, how many of them have involved a person with my educational background?
- What do you like best about the company?

The jovial tone.   This tone creates a mood of trust, approval, and acceptance between interviewee and interviewer. In that environment, many interviewers will give away information or insight that they might withhold from a more aloof interviewee. Humor, or simply good feelings, can be used to create a nonthreatening environment that dissolves nervousness for both parties and increases the chances of a favorable decision from the interviewer.

SAMPLE QUESTIONS USING THE JOVIAL TONE

- I can tell this company really promotes physical fitness and team sports. How do you find time to work?
- I guess we've each had our share of weird bosses. What's your first sign that a boss is weird?
- It's great that you think of your employees as a big, happy family. What happens if a new kid just doesn't fit in?

The urgent tone.   Especially when interviewers drone on about the history of the company, an urgent tone and short, direct questions can turn the interview back on course—and give you a chance to tell why you should be hired. In using the urgent tone, the interviewee need not sound disapproving or hostile, but simply earnest in a desire to get to important matters. Physicians, for example, have honed the urgent question to an art; when patients ramble on, the physician politely but firmly cuts in with a specific question. Interviewers, too, use this tone to test an applicant's ability to shift from a prepared speech.

SAMPLE QUESTIONS USING THE URGENT TONE

- I appreciate your review of company history. But can you sum up for me where you see the company going in the next year?
- I'm happy to talk about past jobs, but let me suggest that one question matters most of all: What can I do for your company?
- I know that my time's almost up for this interview. May I sum up what I consider my major strengths for this position?

The intimate tone. *Interviewer:* "Just between us, this company has an opportunity in the next six months to leap-frog the competition."

Why "just between us"? That air of intimacy, used appropriately, signals the desire of the interviewer or interviewee to speak in an off-the-record, unguarded, and informal way. When used by an interviewer, this tone can sometimes coax the interviewee to reveal more than he should about a particular issue or opinion. Used by the interviewee, this tone can often get the interviewer to relax her questions and relate more openly to the candidate.

SAMPLE QUESTIONS USING THE INTIMATE TONE

- Organizational charts of the company are helpful, but what's your own view on where the action is right now?
- I've had the official tour of the company, but I would really appreciate your unofficial perspective on what I can do to get this job.
- You seem to be a person who knows a lot about personalities in the company. Can you give me any advice on my interview this afternoon with Mr. Devlin?

Your choice of tone determines to a large degree the kind of response you will receive from others.

INSIGHT 26

Your Turn

Write about a time when you used one of the verbal tones described in this chapter to achieve a particular purpose in conversation. What were the circumstances? How did you decide which tone to use? How did things turn out?

_____

_____

_____

Volume

How loud do you speak as an interviewee? You may not know. Interviewees often misjudge their volume, usually erring in the belief that they are speaking too loudly—when in fact the interviewer may be having trouble hearing what they are saying. Measure your own volume habits against the following facts:

- *Most interviewees do not adjust their volume for the size of the room or their distance from the interviewer.* Interviews in corporations occur in large board rooms, offices, and virtual closets, all with varying acoustics and seating arrangements. If the interviewee drones on without a change in volume to match these changing locations, the results can be negative indeed.

- *Interviewers usually will not tell you to speak up.* The politics and etiquette of interviewing are such that interviewers will sit through a low-volume interview without giving a hint that they can't hear much of what's being said. Learn to "hear" the silent protests of interviewers about a too-low volume by noting squinting eyes, knitted eyebrows, and a forward-tilted sitting position. These are signs that you should raise your volume.

- *Too much volume may be interpreted by interviewers as pushiness or hostility.* Speaking too loudly can shorten an interview and cause even the best-intentioned interviewer to wilt. Through their childhood years, many interviewers have associated a raised voice with reprimands and anger. That long association carries over to the interview room. If you've been told by friends that you have an unusually strong voice, watch for signs on the part of the interviewer that you are coming on too forcefully. These signs can include the interviewer's efforts to increase the distance between you and to play with barriers (books, files, etc.) that separate you.

INSIGHT 27	Under the influence of nerves, interviewees are often unaware of the volume level of their speaking, whether too loud or too soft.

Your Turn

Evaluate the volume of your own speaking in interviews. Do you speak too softly, too loudly, or about right? More important, how will you discover if your judgment about your own volume level is correct?

_____

_____

_____

Pace

Interviewer: "I don't think she was interested in what we were discussing. The whole interview just seemed like a ritual to her."

This judgment is made daily through the country as interviewees blitz through their "prepared answers" to expected interview questions. The obligatory remarks about wanting to work for the company are committed to rote and delivered at break-neck speed.

Why? Because interviewees mistakenly assume that their glibness gains points from the interviewer. Although they may have made these "interview speeches" many times, interviewees forget that interviewers want to hear and understand what they have to say. Pace, the rate at which words are said, influences how the interviewer handles the interview and evaluates its outcome. When the pace it too rapid, interviewers miss important answers and draw conclusions about the candidate's lack of sincerity and interest. When the pace is too slow, interviewers grow bored with the conversation and the candidate.

For general interviewing purposes, interviewees should use a pace just slightly slower than usual conversation. (This slower pace will emphasize the importance of the occasion and will help to compensate for the inevitable tendency to speed up under the influence of nerves.) To get a feel for this pace, interviewees can bracket off a passage of approximately 200 words. Read this passage in one minute to hear a moderately slow conversational pace.

Vary the pace of your speaking as a way of emphasizing main topics (using a slower pace) and de-emphasizing less important information (which can be dispatched at a faster pace to prevent boredom).

Speaking too quickly or too slowly sends powerful signals to listeners. They can conclude that the speaker either does not care much for their attention or is willing to abuse their time by saying words too slowly.

INSIGHT 28

Your Turn

Does the pace of your speaking vary? When and how? In an interview situation, how can you keep yourself from speaking too quickly or too slowly? Explain your response.

_____

_____

_____

Emphasis

Particularly when you've been through the "script" of a typical interview many times, you may tend to drone, with your key points blended indistinguishably with less important points. The unrelieved sameness of such speech conveys lack of interest to the interviewer.

Emphasis can be marked by increased volume, higher pitch, and distinct pauses. Interviewees can bring life back into their answers, comments, and questions by restoring appropriate emphasis to four areas:

Key Words

Interviewees who prepare for interviews can target certain words for highlighting. In the following passage, notice how much more persuasive the words are when emphasis is placed on the italicized words (You may want to read the passage first without emphasis and then a second time with emphasis on the italicized words.)

> I'm sure the company *understands* that there are many tensions that come with accepting a new job. I'm saying good-bye to *close friends* and moving on to new *challenges.* I'm selling a family *home* and looking for a new *neighborhood* and new *schools*. That's why it means *so much* to me that the company gives *special attention* to relocation, helping my family and me adjust to a *new* work environment and a *new* city.

Beginnings of New Topics

We all tend to remember best what we hear at the beginning of conversations. What occurs later, especially in the middle, is often forgotten. Use this natural inclination to your advantage as an interviewee by loading the "front end" of answers and explanations with important, emphasized words. The interviewer may forget up to 75 percent of what you say during the interview—but the 25 percent retained will no doubt be from key ideas you placed at the beginning of your responses.

Summaries

In the middle of a long response even the best interviewer's eyes may start to glaze over. Pull attention back to your main point by a summary sentence, emphasized by raised volume and appropriate pauses. Following are four ways to mark such summaries:

"Here's my point."
"So let me make sure I understand you so far."
"To sum up before moving on, . . . "
"Bottom line, here's the key point."

Conclusions

Our last impression is often as powerful as our first impression. For that reason, interviewees practice placing special emphasis on their final words to an interviewer. Unfortunately, too many interviews end with the candidate mumbling, "No, I guess I don't have any questions." Instead, interviewees should express their appreciation for the interview and recap, in a very brief way, their earnest reasons for wanting the job.

Techniques for creating emphasis make our speaking clear, memorable, and interesting.   **INSIGHT 29**

Your Turn

Review the techniques for emphasis described in this chapter. Which techniques do you already use? Which do you need to work on to perfect your ability to create emphasis in your speaking?

_____

_____

_____

_____

_____

_____

Pauses

People great and small pause frequently in some of the most important communication experiences of life: accepting the Nobel Prize, proposing marriage, or explaining the facts of life to the kids. Pauses serve at least three functions. First, they give our listeners time to consider our words (and hence act as a signal that we think the words are worth special consideration). Second, they communicate our sincerity in giving the impression that we carefully consider what we just said or are about to say. Finally, they set off one set of words from surrounding words as an aid to the listener, who is attempting to order and make meaning out of what we're saying.

In giving responses to interviewers, candidates can use pauses to create a feeling of spontaneity in what otherwise might be a dry conversation. Just as a pause creates a bit of suspense, culmination, or interruption in music, so a pause in speaking helps to create the "music" of pleasing conversation.

INSIGHT 30	*A pause allows both the listener and the speaker to reflect for a brief moment on the importance of what has been said and to think ahead to what will follow.*

Your Turn

Why do you think so many speakers are afraid to insert full pauses in their speaking (but instead fill every potential pause with "um," "ah," "you know," or some other sound)? How do you plan to use pauses? What is your plan for using pauses more effectively?

_____

_____

_____

_____

_____

_____

Articulation

Words have to be said clearly and distinctly if they are to be understood. As an interviewee, steer clear of the three traditional enemies to articulated speech:

1. Words spoken quickly, often in excitement, tend to run together. *Example:* Wudjawannadayortwotatritacallim? (Would you want a day or two to try to call him?)

2. Words at the ends of sentences are often articulated poorly. Once an idea is partially expressed in words, our minds rush ahead to the next idea and often do not do justice to the final words of the sentence. To check your performance in this regard, tape-record a practice interview session. Listen to your strong, distinct sentence beginnings and compare them with your sentence closings. If you hear your voice drop in volume and your articulation begin to slur, you have the "end-of-sentence slump." Jot down several of your sentences from the practice interview, then read them into the tape recorder with appropriate emphasis and articulation on the end portions of your sentences. Notice the difference? Your interviewer will too.

3. The sounds b/p, m/n, t/d, f/s, and th/sh are often articulated poorly. We're all guilty occasionally of sliding over these consonantal sounds, particularly when talking quickly in casual conversation. Interviews, of course, share many of the qualities of casual conversation and therefore are full of these articulation potholes. To brush up your articulation skills, read the following sentences several times with careful attention to the articulation of each sound. Don't let word sounds run together, especially if meaning is at stake (as in "night rate" vs. "nitrate").

- Bob will be pleased to bill Paul for a better brand of pills.
- Tip big porters up at the pub beside the Pacific Boat Barn.
- Mention my name, Manny, and maybe no more mandates will come.
- One man may name no more than one nominee.
- Brad taught Dot how to do two double-digit totals at one time.
- Tom's two dates don't demand total devotion to domestic details.
- A safe, soft thought is suited for those with something that seems thrilling.
- Thorsen Forest sent his spouse forth for the frosh/soph shot put.

By careful articulation you can give the interviewer a better chance to understand what you're saying and give you credit for it.

INSIGHT 31	*An inability to make out what a speaker is saying because of poor articulation frustrates listeners and may cause them to oppose perspectives and positions being advanced by the speaker.*

Your Turn

Work through the articulation exercise in this chapter. Which items are particularly challenging for you? Once you have identified these, develop a plan to master these aspects of articulation over the next few weeks.

_____

_____

_____

_____

_____

_____

Pitch

Like music, our voices rise and fall naturally in coordination with our meaning and level of excitement. In interview situations, however, too many interviewees turn into "Johnny One-Note."

A tape recording of a practice interview session will clearly reveal any pitch problems you have. Some interviewees discover they are "Gravel Gerties," and need to speak "up and out," raising their chin a bit as a way of raising the pitch of their voice. Other interviewees hit a high note and hold it, producing by the end of the interview a sound effect not unlike fingernails on the chalkboard. In this case, drink some water, relax the vocal apparatus, and speak more calmly. These techniques will lower the pitch of the voice into a more natural range.

INSIGHT 32	*A pleasant speaking voice uses a variety of pitches to add interest and "flow" to speaking.*

Your Turn

Write down your own assessment of the pitch levels you typically use in business speaking (such as an interview situation). Next, ask a friend to review what you have written. Does your friend agree with your estimate of your own pitch levels? If the friend points out a problem with pitch, develop a plan to speak with more variety in pitch.

Summing Up

The work of upgrading verbal skills is much like remodeling a house. For the sake of those living there, it's much better to take one room at a time. In the same way, you should target one or two aspects of the way you speak for improvement over the next few weeks. At first you may feel self-conscious as you speak. But with patience and practice, your early failures will turn into more and more steady successes. As you achieve your goals, set new targets. The dividends of this routine will surprise you—new professionalism in the way you present yourself and your thoughts in interviews; a new respect evident in the way interviewers treat you; and much less frustration in correcting, restating, and clarifying your intended messages.

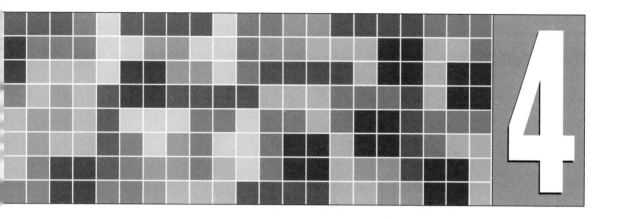

Nonverbal Techniques for Interviewing

GOALS

- Grasp that nonverbal signals accompanying one's speech are equally important in conveying impressions.

- Learn to manage nonverbal techniques to advantage in interview situations.

- Review the primary contributors to the nonverbal messages one sends.

This chapter turns the spotlight on often-ignored aspects of your performance as an interviewee: the impressions you create (or fail to create) by eye contact, posture, gestures, facial expressions, dress, and other nonverbal forms of communication. These are the "hidden communicators" that we sometimes overlook in our eagerness to say the right thing in interviews. What we *show* by our nonverbal communication turns out to be at least as important as what we *tell* in determining our interview success.

Recently a group of railroad managers participated in an interesting interview experiment. In groups of three, they watched a five-minute videotape of a selection interview. The camera showed only the seated interviewee, both face and body. More important, the sound was turned off. Based solely on what they saw, the teams were asked to reach consensus on an approximate "script" for the interview—whether it was going well or poorly, whether the candidate was enthused or uninterested, and whether the candidate was likely to get the job. Here's a portion of one team's impressions:

> The candidate seems to like the interviewer. She smiles and responds in a friendly way. But then something goes wrong. Maybe she got stuck on a question. She shows signs of frustration and confusion. Physically she seems to shrink back in her chair, as if she is trying to withdraw from the conversation. Her expression looks pained. At the end of the interview, her eyes are pinched and her lips are tight. She probably didn't get the job—and didn't want it.

Once this script was written, the videotape was replayed, this time with the sound on. To the surprise of no one, the group had correctly "read" the progress of the interview solely by observing the interviewee's nonverbal signals.

What we show with our eyes, expressions, posture, gestures, and other nonverbal signals is not a minor commentary on what we say. To the contrary, nonverbal messages are usually more influential than verbal messages in communicating our thoughts and feelings. The dominance of nonverbal over verbal signals can be demonstrated by a simple experiment. Touch your forefinger to your thumb to form an "O" and ask another individual to do the same. Next, say to the individual, "Place this 'O' on your chin." But as you give these verbal instructions place your own joined finger and thumb onto your cheek, not your chin. The vast majority of individuals will predictably follow your nonverbal lead—what you show—rather than your verbal directions—what you say.

Why do we believe what we see more than what we hear? Probably we have learned from childhood on that people exercise less conscious control over their nonverbal signals than over their words. They give away their real messages and motives by a look in the eyes, a tension in the facial muscles, or a twitch on the lips even when their words have been carefully rehearsed. The mere words "I have no idea how the fender got dented!" didn't work for us as teenagers because our nonverbal cues were simultaneously screaming out our guilt.

| **INSIGHT 33** | *Because they seem less rehearsed and planned, our nonverbal signals are often taken as a true reflection of our feelings and intentions by others.* |

Your Turn

Write about a time when your words (verbal behavior) differed substantially from the signals you were sending nonverbally. Which did others tend to believe? How did things turn out?

_____

_____

_____

_____

_____

_____

CAN NONVERBAL BEHAVIOR BE CONTROLLED?

But can we grab hold of our nonverbal signals just as we have learned to control our words? For most of us, the answer is "yes and no." Yes, we can become aware of our nonverbal signals and take steps to bring them into harmony with our verbal signals. Nevertheless, feelings have a way of slipping out despite our best efforts—as Shakespeare said, "Truth will out." We will never (and perhaps should never) become such perfect puppet masters of our nonverbal behavior that not a look, frown, nor twitch occurs without our willing it.

If complete control of nonverbal signals is not a practical goal, strive for the following:

- Sensitize yourself to the language of the nonverbal messages you send and receive.
- Understand the confusion that results when you send mixed verbal and nonverbal messages.
- Coordinate your message sending so that both verbal and nonverbal techniques cooperate in creating clear meaning.

Even though we cannot completely control our nonverbal signals, we can become aware that they matter to the total reception of messages we are trying to send.   **INSIGHT 34**

Your Turn

Which nonverbal signals do you believe are most easy to control? Which are more difficult or even impossible?

Eye Contact

An interviewer welcomes you to the interview room. You glance at this person long enough to shake a hand perfunctorily, then look down to the resume and application form you hold in your moist fingers. When you are asked the first interview question, you look down at your hands, then at the wall.

The eyes! That's where you will find and convey more telling information than from any other source. In the first 10 seconds of an interview encounter, the eyes begin to communicate at least five crucial bits of information:

1. how nervous you are
2. how friendly you are
3. how confident you are
4. how socially skilled you are
5. how alert you are

Don't misunderstand. We are not suggesting that the ultimate impression you make on interviewers or others depends solely on your eye contact. How simple interviewing would be if that were so! But you do create first impressions in your initial opportunities for eye contact. Others often use these impressions as hypotheses to be tried out and proven during the interview. In other words, interviewers look for additional information to bolster initial impressions.

Few people are as adept at eye contact as they should be. The reasons are many. Some may wish to postpone a person-to-person relationship with the interviewer as long as possible and therefore withhold any eye-to-eye bond. Others believe that they can think better and answer better by keeping the eyes focused on a wall, a window, or the carpet. And for others a natural tendency toward shyness takes over. The eyes attempt to "hide out" during the interview even if the body can't.

In the face of all these understandable and quite human excuses for poor eye contact, interviewees committed to their success will challenge themselves to establish and maintain good eye contact because of three dividends:

1. Good eye contact helps us send and receive complete messages in which feelings join with ideas.

2. Good eye contact keeps both the interviewee and interviewer in the "now," the moment at hand. Nothing is more discouraging in an interview than a rambling response. Eye contact keeps us from drifting away from the listener's attention and interest.

3. Good eye contact encourages relaxation and sincerity. Especially when eye contact communicates friendliness and respect, both parties to the conversation begin to shed their defenses and relate openly as individuals.

Eye contact is one of the most important factors in nonverbal communication because it signals our intention to have a direct, interested relationship with others.   **INSIGHT 35**

Your Turn

What is your own track record with regard to eye contact? Are you good at it in public speaking situations? When do you find it most difficult to practice? Write a brief plan you can use to become more skilled at eye contact.

_____

_____

_____

_____

How to Achieve Good Eye Contact

We are all superb at eye contact at one time or another. But how to do it consistently when it matters—there's the rub. Begin with yourself. Look into your own eyes in a mirror. The first thoughts and possible awkwardness have to be discarded. Get to the main event: what you see in your own eyes. This activity may feel strange, but rest assured that it is practiced regularly by your favorite television or film star.

You may not be sure what you see when you look into your eyes in the mirror. So act a bit. First, turn on a bit of anxiety. Notice how your eyes communicate your sense of foreboding. Now switch to warm, relaxed eye contact—the look of laid-back contentment. What a difference! Try keen, focused attention.

Getting to know and respect the communicative power of your own eyes gives you confidence to use them for assertive eye contact. You know the messages that you're capable of sending. In effect, you know what the other person (or interviewer!) is seeing.

Once we turn away from the mirror to establish eye contact with a real person, of course, the game of nonverbal communication becomes much more complex. Now we not only serve up signals of feelings through our eyes but we also have someone returning the serve with their own eye contact. We don't always get back the same kinds of signals we send. For example, we may send out signals of sincere, patient interest. We get back eye contact that communicates frustration and impatience. Now what?

This moment—when we receive the first reaction to our eye contact—is crucial for interviewees. We are naturally tempted to respond in kind: If the interviewer sends a look of frustration, we will visually echo it in our look of anxiety or confusion, as if inquiring what is wrong. Once this process begins, it takes on a life of its own, with each party responding to what she thinks she sees in the other's eyes. Rapport falls to pieces.

To prevent this devolution of first impressions, be sure enough of your own feelings (as projected through your eyes) to hold on for a few moments. Resolve to maintain your sincere, caring eye contact no matter what the other person "sends" you in his own eye contact during the period of first impressions.

Natural eye contact that promotes comfortable conversation differs from a stare in three ways:

1. Stares look at another person; natural eye contact looks into another person.
2. Stares hold on like a pit bull; natural eye contact breaks away occasionally to increase social comfort for both parties.
3. Stares are fixed in one expression; natural eye contact allows a variety of feelings to develop and express themselves.

> *Eye contact must appear natural; otherwise, it backfires by making listeners feel they are being stared at.*   **INSIGHT 36**

Your Turn

Write about a person who is superb in the skill of eye contact. Next, write a contrasting description about a person who is terrible in the skill of eye contact. What personal characteristics seem to account for this difference between individuals? What impact has their varying skill levels in eye contact had on their ability to relate well to others?

_____

_____

_____

_____

An Eye Contact Experiment

Convince a friend that his or her cooperation in this experiment will be important to your interviewing success. Find a quiet spot where the two of you can simply look into one another's eyes for about two minutes. (This isn't a game of stare-down; you have permission to blink.) Watch for feelings as they develop and change. If you break down in laughter, try it again. After your two minutes of eye contact, talk about what you felt and what you perceived the other person felt. Check your perceptions. Were you right—or were you drawing conclusions based on eye contact that the other person found surprising or inaccurate? This experiment is a quick, memorable way to learn much about the power of eye contact.

In addition to encouraging rapport, eye contact can serve three additional functions in interviewing:

1. *Encouraging the interviewer to clarify a question or give a helpful response.* You don't have to say a word. Your direct look of interest and attention, combined with a short silent pause, signals the interviewer that you need additional information or feedback. Often this "silent inquiry" is preferable to a verbal request on your part ("Could you repeat the question?").

2. *Indicating your appreciation, pleasure, or approval during the interview process.* It's often difficult to pay the interviewer a compliment; such explicit

praise can seem self-serving when put into words ("I'm really enjoying my conversation with you!"). But eye contact that communicates your favorable feelings can be a nonverbal way of saying "this is great!"

3. *Motivating the interviewer to be straightforward with you.* People tend to get to the point when you hold them in direct eye contact. They often allow themselves to ramble when your gaze moves to the ceiling or wall.

INSIGHT 37	*We are often "blind" to the movement and position of our own eyes, particularly in situations that stimulate nervousness.*

Your Turn

Ask a few friends to give you an honest assessment of your skills in eye contact. Use this information to develop a plan for continued improvement.

_____

_____

_____

Posture and Body Movement

What attitudes and feelings do you associate with each of the postures in the figure below? Twenty University of Southern California students were asked this question. Their most frequent answers appear beneath each picture.

| discouraged, tired | shifty, sarcastic | unmotivated, insensitive | nervous, over-eager |

Your answers may be quite similar to those of the USC students. After all, we all have been schooled by the same teacher—everyday life. We share general impressions of how confident people sit and stand—and, by contrast, how insecure or nervous people sit and stand. What we do not usually know, ironically, is how we ourselves sit, stand, and move during an interview. Our senses are directed outward, not inward. Lacking mirrors or videotape cameras, we have little direct experience of what we really look like in action. (This may explain the general distaste of being videotaped. For many people, such an experience is the first time they have watched themselves from various angles.)

Posture and movement are capable of conveying confidence, energy, and enthusiasm—or their opposites.   **INSIGHT 38**

Your Turn

Evaluate your own posture and movement, both when you are sitting (as in an interview situation) and when you are standing (as in a public speaking situation). Once you have written your own evaluation, check your impressions with a friend. Then develop a plan for improving these important aspects of your nonverbal communication.

_____

_____

_____

_____

_____

_____

Learning to See Ourselves as Others See Us

The poet Robert Burns said it well: "Oh, that someone the gift would give us / To see ourselves as others see us!" Initially, self-observation can be painful, but it provides the best route toward changing ineffective habits.

If you have access to a videotape camera, arrange a practice interview session so that you can observe yourself in action. Pay particular attention to your various sitting positions, the frequency with which you shift in your chair, your posture, your hand and arm movements, and your crossed or un-crossed legs. Take notes on the nonverbal signals you appear to be sending by your posture and movement during the interview.

Don't be misled by popularized treatments of "what crossed legs mean" or "what your hands are revealing about you." No single movement in itself means anything at all in an absolute way. Body movements dur-ing interviews are much more like a ballet, with suggested but not defi-nite meanings. The important thing is for you to locate the meaning you associate with certain postures and movements. What signals do you feel you are sending by playing with a ring while you speak or twisting at a piece of hair? Your conclusions about your nonverbal signals will be a strong influence in determining what to change in your posture and movements.

If you don't have access to a videotape camera, ask a friend to watch you during the course of a practice interview. Ask your friend to jot down ob-servational (not critical) notes about your posture and body movement. Re-view those notes, asking for impressions your friend formed during the interview. As an example of this kind of exchange, the following transcript is an observation written for a San Francisco job seeker:

> You looked fresh and professional at first. You sat comfortably and deeply in your chair. But as you became more animated in conversation, you kept repositioning yourself in the chair, as if you were really uncomfortable. Your movements were abrupt and jerky—leaning forward suddenly, then pushing yourself back. Toward the end of the interview you slumped back in your chair with your arms crossed. I thought that either you were discouraged or you had your mind made up. That position seemed to shut down communication with the interviewer.

Hands are particularly revealing of feeling. See if you agree with the general attitudes or feelings suggested by the hand positions in the fol-lowing figure:

 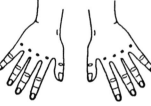

assertion, anger   pleading   conciliation, calming   consideration, reflection

Many interviewees hide their hands during the interview session, keeping them below the level of the table or tucking them alongside their legs. In so doing, they fail to make use of a powerful communication tool. If you are self-conscious about your hands while speaking, try the following recipe for effective gestures.

Step One.   Keep your hands front and center, not under the table. When you are not gesturing, lay your hands comfortably on the table.

Step Two.   As you begin to speak, allow your hands to move naturally with your words. (You do so unconsciously when speaking to friends.) In this way, you use your hands to punctuate your words with visual support. You add physical feeling and emphasis to what you say.

Step Three.   Extend your range of gestures by "counting on your fingers"—that is, enumerating points by putting up one finger at a time or touching fingers in order with the other hand. Use other gestures you find comfortable and appropriate, such as the "eraser" movement with your hand, in which you briefly rub your fingers in the air as if erasing a previous comment or misunderstanding.

Step Four.   When you're comfortable gesturing with a single hand, raise both hands into motion. A good starting gesture, particularly when answering an interview question, is the "basketball" position. Simply hold your hands open and apart as if holding a basketball. Talk to the interviewer through your opened hands, letting them drop at a natural point in conversation.

Step Five.   Now go for the big time with full arm gestures. Watch yourself and others in ordinary, spirited conversation for examples of these large movements. Interviewees who gesture freely and naturally tend to score well in interviews of all kinds. Interviewers pay compliments such as "you kept conversation lively," "you seemed very involved," and "you appeared committed and energetic." These impressions are the dividends earned from a small investment of time and attention to movements that come naturally in everyday speaking—but may be forgotten under the influence of nerves during an interview.

We use our hands and arms to signal affection, self-defense, astonishment, devotion, and a wide range of other states.   **INSIGHT 39**

Write an assessment of your hand and arm gestures. In what areas are you already strong? Where do you need improvement? Create a plan to make that improvement happen.

Facial Expressions

More than one interviewee has come out of a job-seeking interview almost in tears. "You should have seen the interviewer's face," an interviewee complains. "He seemed disgusted with everything I said."

Second only to our eyes, our facial expressions reveal more about our feelings and attitudes than any other nonverbal signal. In thinking about the impressions you create by your facial expressions, consider your options in each of the following areas:

Lips. Pressed tight, lips can communicate impatience, frustration, and nervous discomfort. Touching the tongue to the upper lip can signal hesitation, suspicion, or doubt. Pursing the lips (assuming a kiss isn't in order) can communicate shrewd, calculating evaluation. Biting the lower lip often signals tension over a perceived mistake or faux pas. Your goal should be to make sure the signals you are sending with your lips are indeed the messages you mean to communicate.

Chin. More than is usually recognized, the chin plays a prominent part in setting the tone for interpersonal communication. A jutting, defiant chin, raised imperiously, can communicate the interviewee's defensiveness. A buried chin can signal embarrassment, insecurity, or suspicion. A "chewing jaw" sometimes indicates impatience with the conversation. Or it can communicate to the interviewer that questions are uncomfortable for the interviewee.

Cheeks. Puffing out one's cheeks, often with a burst of air, can communicate weariness, incredulity, or frustration. A tongue wandering about the inner contours of the cheek can give the interviewer the impression that what the interviewee says isn't entirely what she means.

Eyebrows and forehead.   This single muscular plate operates as one unit, with strong visual effect and potential for nonverbal meaning. Interviewees commonly make the mistake of lowering their eyebrows and knitting their foreheads as a sign of intense concentration. The appearance, unfortunately, is identical to a frown and may be interpreted as such by interviewers.

Ears.   Thankfully, the ears have practically nothing to say nonverbally in interviews. Why they are the constant prey of marauding fingers is difficult to say. In Italy, the "ear-pull" has a defined meaning: "I'm on to you." But in the United States, ear pulling, ear cleaning, and other forms of ear massage during the interview are simply bad habits.

> *Especially in the close contact of interview situations, the signals sent by our faces are crucial to rapport with the interviewer.*   **INSIGHT 40**

Your Turn

Watch yourself in a mirror as you practice giving answers to some of the interview questions in this book. Jot down notes on what you like about the signals sent by your face and also on what you would like to change. Make specific plans to change what you can about facial messages that are not serving you well.

_____

_____

_____

_____

_____

Dress

Despite the assertions of "dress for success" books and articles, there is no firm evidence that any one "look" or power suit (for men or women) is right for all interview occasions. In choosing what to wear for the important occasion of an interview, be guided by several principles:

- your own good sense and good taste.
- the typical business dress you have observed at the company where you are interviewing. (**A note of caution:** if the company culture

encourages very casual dress, you may still want to present yourself in more conservative clothes at the interview so as not to seem presumptuous that you are already "one of the gang.")

■ restrained use of accessories or personal jewelry that calls attention to itself and distracts focus away from who you are and what you are saying.

Like the rest of your nonverbal communicators, dress can be controlled so that it helps to convey the image and personality you desire in your interview.

| **INSIGHT 41** | *Appropriate dress communicates our sensitivity to the place, occasion, and human relationships in the interview situation.* |

Your Turn

Describe an interview you may want to seek in the future. Tell how you would dress for this interview and explain why.

_____

_____

_____

_____

_____

_____

Summing Up

What people see in us is at least as potent in creating impressions as what people hear from us. Although physical gestures happen in large part without our conscious planning or control, we are nevertheless able to develop many nonverbal techniques (such as better eye contact or more expressive gestures) and to tone down physical movements or expressions that may be sending messages at variance with our intentions.

What to Do When Interview Questions Turn Illegal

GOALS

- Identify areas where interview questions are in danger of violating state and federal laws.

- Understand the rationale for prohibiting such questions.

- Develop personal strategies for handling such illegal questions if they occur in one of your interviews.

You're probably aware that interviewers are not supposed to ask you certain questions. This chapter updates you on the "Fatal Five" areas of special sensitivity in selection interviewing. The goal is twofold: to point out these illegal areas of questions, and to suggest strategic ways to handle them if they occur in your interview.

Our aim here is not to turn you into a "legal eagle" on constant alert for any cause to accuse or sue an interviewing company. In truth, many instances of illegal interview questions (such as, "Are you married?") occur in the course of ordinary getting-to-know-you small talk during an interview and aren't intended by the interviewer as an intrusion into your privacy. But innocent or not, illegal interview questions can land a company in court when a job seeker claims discrimination in the interview process.

Learning to avoid illegal questions as an interviewer and handling them well as an interviewee is the focus of this chapter.

WHO MAKES THE RULES FOR INTERVIEW QUESTIONS?

No single federal, state, or local agency or court defines for all cases which interview questions are legal or illegal. Instead, a plethora of court rulings, legislative decisions, agency regulations, and constitutional laws combine to produce the often confusing and frequently changing list of what you can and can't ask a job applicant.

HOW TO ANSWER DIFFICULT QUESTIONS

Following are our suggestions for some of the more difficult areas in which the employer must exercise caution when asking questions—and you must be equally careful in how or if you answer.

INSIGHT 42	*The list of illegal questions grows according to court precedents and legislative mandates.*

Your Turn

Have you or someone you know faced illegal interview questions? How did you respond? If you faced the experience again, would you respond in the same way? If you have no such experience with or knowledge of illegal interview questions, discuss how you would handle such questions if they occur in a future interview.

_____

_____

_____

_____

Marital Circumstances

Courts have ruled that it's none of the company's business how many children an applicant has; whether he or she is married, single, divorced, or engaged; whether the applicant plans to become pregnant at any time in the future; how the applicant's spouse or partner feels about overnight travel; or what plans the applicant has made for child care during the workday.

Managers stumble into trouble in this area when making small talk, especially of a disclosing or "sharing" nature with the candidate. Manager: "My wife and I have lived here for about 10 years. We love it—especially the school system. Do you have kids?" Innocent? Of course. But if relations turn litigious, the manager will have to admit in court that he inquired about children as part of the selection interview.

Appropriate Questions

- Do you have responsibilities or commitments that will prevent you from meeting specified work schedules?
- Do you anticipate any absences from work on a regular basis? If so, please explain the circumstances.

What to Do

If you are asked an illegal question in this area, you can give a general response, said graciously: "I would prefer to stick to job-related questions." Or you can be more pointed: "Are children a requirement for this position?" And, of course, you can always decide simply to play along, but as minimally as possible: "Yes, we have one child. Shall we talk about your requirements for this position?"

Women are often asked illegal questions having to do with marital status or family responsibilities; these same questions are rarely asked of male candidates. In this way, women face discrimination in the hiring process. **INSIGHT 43**

Your Turn

No matter what the law, do you believe an employer should have the right to hire with an eye toward a candidate's family responsibilities? Argue your position pro or con.

_____

_____

_____

Age

To prevent age discrimination in hiring, courts have disallowed these sorts of questions: "How old are you?" "In what year were you born?" "When did you graduate from high school?" and so forth. You do have the right to ask whether the applicant meets the legal age requirements for work in your city or state.

Managers stray into trouble here when they talk about the average age of their workforce in relation to the candidate: "Our typical employee is probably 8 to 10 years older than you. Do you anticipate problems managing people older than yourself?" You can imagine the later court scene. *Manager:* "But, Your Honor, I never asked her age!" *Candidate/plaintiff:* "My age seemed to be one of his key concerns about my ability to manage." Verdict goes to the plaintiff, with back pay, damages, and court costs.

Appropriate Questions

- Do you meet the minimum age requirement set by law in our area? If hired, can you produce proof of your age?
- If you are a minor, can you provide proof of age in the form of a work permit or certificate of age?

What to Do

If asked an illegal question having to do with your age, you can respond, with a smile: "Age has never been a consideration for me in my work life." Or you can turn the knife a bit: "Is my age being considered as part of my application?" And, of course, you can simply answer, if you wish: "I'm 27, but my age hasn't been a consideration in past jobs."

INSIGHT 44   *Certain jobs seem predefined for certain ages, for example, servers at a fast-food restaurant. Federal and state law makes such automatic assumptions about age illegal when applied to the hiring process.*

Your Turn

List six jobs, then for each jot down what you believe to be the usual age range for people who hold that job. Now examine your findings. Which jobs actually require people within a certain age range and which could use employees from a much broader age range? In your opinion, what is the source of age discrimination?

Disabilities

Companies are forbidden by law from asking an applicant if he or she has mental or physical disabilities. Nor can they inquire about the nature or severity of disabilities, no matter how apparent they seem in the hiring process. Any physical or mental requirements a company establishes as a prerequisite for hiring must be based on "business necessity" and the safe performance of the job.

Managers are misled here by their best intentions: "We have many people with disabilities working for us and we support their needs in every way possible. For example, we could overcome the problem you have with your hands by giving you an automated speech recognition word processor." If the candidate with disabilities does not get the job, the manager's assumptions about the candidate's typing abilities could come back to haunt in an expensive way.

Appropriate Questions

- You are *invited*, not required, to indicate whether and to what extent you may have physical or mental disabilities. We want you to know in advance, however, that any information you disclose is voluntary. This information is sought only to remedy discrimination and provide opportunities for people with disabilities. All information you disclose will be kept confidential. If you choose not to provide information, that choice will in no way affect your chances for being hired.
- Will you be able to carry out in a safe manner all job assignments necessary for this position?

What to Do

If you are asked an illegal question having to do with disabilities, you can refer the interviewer to Americans with Disabilities Act (ADA) guidelines:

"I believe that under current ADA law you can't make this issue a part of the hiring process." Or you can take the edge off a bit with a general answer: "I know of nothing that will prevent me from fulfilling the job requirements of this position."

INSIGHT 45   *The only question at issue with a person with disabilities is the question that must be asked of all applicants: Can you do the job?*

Your Turn

Imagine a scenario in which a person with disabilities applied to you, the manager, for a job in a factory setting. Write down the questions you would use in the interview as you explored this person's ability to do the job.

_____

_____

_____

_____

Sex and Physical Appearance

An employer cannot ask questions about the person's gender unless the job specifications strictly require either a male or a female. The burden of proof is on the employer to demonstrate that only a man or a woman can do the job. Employers should beware: Courts and the Equal Employment Opportunity Commission have interpreted very narrowly the notion that only one gender can perform a particular job. In addition, employers should avoid questions about the person's physical appearance, including height, weight, grooming, and dress, unless these bear clearly upon job requirements.

Again, a manager's small talk in the job interview is the unhappy hunting ground for mistakes in this area of questioning. *Manager to a woman applicant:* "We have a fitness facility here at the plant. But you seem to be pretty fit already." Oops.

Appropriate Question

■ We want you to know that both men and women are being considered equally for this position. As you understand the job requirements, are you aware of any circumstances or conditions that may prevent you from successfully performing the job?

What to Do

If quizzed about matters of gender or physical appearance, you can respond in a general way: "I'm fully prepared to take on these job responsibilities, and I don't think gender or appearance plays a role." Or you can return the question with a question: "Are gender and appearance being considered as part of this hiring process?" These responses need not be said in a snarlish way (though the interviewer may well deserve your anger). You can preserve your chances for the job by handling the questions professionally.

Physical appearance and gender are often "hidden discriminators" used to disqualify otherwise well-suited applicants from job consideration.   **INSIGHT 46**

Your Turn

Briefly describe your own observations with regard to gender and appearance in hiring. Do some people get jobs, or fail to get jobs, primarily on the basis of their physical appearance (pro or con) or gender? Explain your response and feelings on this matter.

_____

_____

_____

_____

_____

_____

Citizenship and National Origin

A company cannot legally inquire into the applicant's place of birth, ancestry, native language, spouse's or parents' birthplace, or residence. Nor can an employer ask directly, "Are you a U. S. citizen?" or "Do you have naturalization papers?" Prior to the decision to hire, these questions may tend to reveal racial or ethnic factors that may bias the employer. Companies should request names of *persons* to notify in case of an emergency rather than specifying *relatives*. Employers should not require that the applicant's photograph be submitted prior to the hiring decision.

Managers often misstep into this pitfall when inquiring about a candidate's second language capability. *Manager:* "You say on your resume that you speak Spanish fluently. Did you grow up in Mexico?" A person's land of birth cannot be grounds for a hiring decision. Clearly, this question strays into legally hazardous areas.

Appropriate Questions

- Can you, after employment, provide verification of your legal right to work in the United States?
- Do you have language abilities other than English that may be useful in performing this job successfully?
- After hiring, are you aware that a photograph may be required for identification?

What to Do

If asked about your national origin, you can answer "My family history and heritage are getting us off the topic, don't you think? I would rather talk about job requirements." Or you can be more direct: "I assume that where my parents came from isn't one of the requirements for this job."

INSIGHT 47   *Employers who do not know about a person's ethnic or national background are less likely to use that information in a prejudicial way.*

Your Turn

Pick a country that is in the news right now for warring acts or some other controversy. Do you feel that an immigrant from that country who has obtained U. S. citizenship will sometimes be discriminated against in the hiring process? How and why? What can be done to prevent such discrimination?

_____

_____

_____

_____

FAREWELL TO SEAT-OF-THE-PANTS INTERVIEWING

In most companies, the days are gone when an untrained interviewer simply asked whatever came to mind. As an applicant, you need to know your rights to be treated equally and fairly in the hiring process. Candidates who are excluded from consideration based on illegal questions have a clear case for legal redress. Here's the bottom-line message for interviewees: Even one illegal question in a hiring interview may put you at a disadvantage for the job. Learn the rules of legal interviewing and, in a gracious but tenacious way, make sure your interviewer plays by them.

A SAMPLER OF ILLEGAL INTERVIEW QUESTIONS

1. Have you ever changed your name? (*potential discrimination based on marital status or national origin*)

2. Are you married, single, or divorced? How many children do you have? Are you pregnant? Do you plan to become pregnant? (*potential discrimination based on sex or marital status*)

3. How old are you? Can you offer proof of your age? (*potential discrimination based on age*)

4. Do you have any disabilities? (*An employer can inquire about physical or mental disabilities that would prevent the applicant from safely or successfully performing specific job duties. The danger in this question is potential discrimination on the basis of disability.*)

5. How tall are you? How much do you weigh? (*potential discrimination based on non–job-related categories*)

6. Do you own your own home? With whom do you live? (*potential discrimination based on sex, marital status, or economic circumstances unrelated to job requirements*)

7. What is your spouse's (partner's) occupation? (*potential discrimination based on sex, marital status, or socioeconomic status unrelated to job requirements*)

8. What kind of credit rating do you have? (*potential discrimination based on race, sex, or socioeconomic status unrelated to job requirements*)

9. Where were you born? What is the birthplace of your nearest relative/father/mother/spouse and so on? (*potential discrimination based on national origin*)

10. Have you ever been arrested? (The employer may ask about convictions related to specific job requirements.) (*potential discrimination based on non–job-related requirements*)

11. List the names of relatives to be notified in the case of emergency. (It is more appropriate for an employer to ask for the names of persons.) (*potential discrimination based on national origin*)

12. List all organizations to which you belong. (The employer may inquire about membership in job-related professional organizations.) (*potential discrimination based on non–job-related requirements*)

13. State your religious preference. (*potential discrimination based on religion*)

14. What type of military discharge do you have? (The employer may inquire about military service relevant to job duties.) (*potential discrimination based on non–job-related requirements*)

Note: Because laws affecting selection interviewing change frequently at all levels of jurisdiction in various locales, we recommend that you review the legality of potential interview areas and questions from time to time with a knowledgeable human resources professional or attorney.

INSIGHT 48

Illegal questions do not always spring from "bad" people. Well-intentioned managers sometimes slip into illegal areas of questioning because they have not been trained by their companies to avoid such areas.

Your Turn

Look over the list of illegal questions in this chapter. Choose three that you believe have the greatest potential to discriminate against people you know. Write about how such discrimination could happen and how it can be prevented.

_____

_____

_____

_____

_____

_____

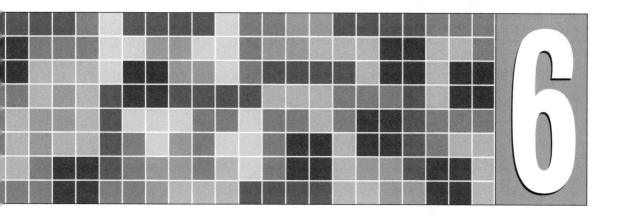

Interview Testing

GOALS

- Recognize the many forms of testing now used as part of the hiring process.

- Understand the techniques and methods of these testing procedures.

- Develop strategies for performing well on tests that accompany selection procedures.

Many job candidates are surprised when an interviewer leads them to a testing room as part of the on-site interview. "I thought they just wanted to talk to me," one job seeker complained. "I ended up spending two hours taking tests and only 30 minutes actually talking to an interviewer." Testing is now an established component in hiring interviews for most Fortune 500 companies and many smaller firms. Tests of various kinds, as described in this chapter, give the company the opportunity to make objective comparisons among candidates and to record evaluation results as part of the documentation justifying the selection of one candidate over another. For job seekers, therefore, preparing for testing is as important as preparing for oral interviewing.

American employers have long wished for and worked for a litmus test that would separate the sheep from the goats in hiring. Some companies have looked with envy at colleges, law schools, business schools, and graduate programs that have based applicant acceptance almost exclusively (no matter what college brochures claimed) on SAT, LSAT, GMAT, and GRE scores, respectively.

Why couldn't companies contract in a similar way with a testing service for an examination that could take the place of laborious and costly interviews? That attempt was, in fact, made beginning in the 1940s with several versions of a test put forward by the Employment Service of the U. S. Department of Labor. The test was called the General Aptitude Test Battery—GATB.

This test seemed ideal as an easy-to-administer, inexpensive way to screen large groups of applicants. By the 1990s, however, the test had run afoul of the Equal Employment Opportunity Commission (EEOC) because it apparently tended to exclude minorities from hiring. The commission approved a complicated scheme of "within-group scoring," or race norming, in which a test taker's score was reported out to potential employers as a percentile within the test taker's racial group. No other score was made available, so employers had no way of comparing test results of applicants from different racial groups.

An epic wrestling match followed between the Department of Justice, which threatened a reverse discrimination lawsuit, and the Department of Labor and EEOC, which made plans to sue several Fortune 500 companies for not race norming their applicants' GATB scores. In the midst of such wrangling, the GATB seemed too risky for employers to bother with. It became obsolete in the early 1990s.

INSIGHT 49	*The idea that one master test will accurately measure all applicants' individual potential for successful work has largely been abandoned by government and private companies.*

Your Turn

What tests have you taken as part of an interview procedure? Did you learn your scores or results? Did you feel the test was a fair predictor of your success as an employee?

THE TEST TO END ALL TESTS

But just as the light was fading from the GATB, many employers spotted a new beacon of hope and help for those who hire: a test that tapped directly into an applicant's deepest character and impulses. Wires touching the skin would record fluctuations in body chemistry in response to probing questions. Without difficult and expensive reference or background checks, the polygraph would tell the employer with some certainty whether a job candidate had ever been fired; had stolen company property in a past position; had experienced personal bankruptcy; or, for that matter, was involved in unusual religious, sexual, or political activity.

Throughout the 1980s, more than two million applicants each year took polygraph tests to qualify for government and corporate jobs. For the private sector, that practice came to an abrupt halt on December 27, 1988, when by Congressional legislation the use of lie detectors was prohibited in most nongovernmental hiring procedures. Congressional representatives, many of whom were lawyers well acquainted with polygraph technology, were persuaded that the commonly accepted accuracy factor of the lie detector—said to be 80 percent—was too low to justify the stigma and unfairness involved in "failing the test." Two of ten applicants, Congress reasoned, should not be summarily banished from employment opportunity because of the inaccuracy of a test technology.

The Senate was particularly impressed by the following statistical analysis of the polygraph, as summarized in *Psychology Today*:

> This problem [of inaccuracy in lie detectors] is compounded in general screening by the fact that most people are honest, which increases the chances that the machine will spot "false positive"—honest people ... who appear crooked. It's a statistical glitch. Consider this: If 20 percent of a pool of 1,000 applicants has something to hide, then there are 800

with clear consciences. If the polygraph is 80 percent accurate, 20 percent of those 800—160 honest applicants—will be falsely accused. And some studies have found that the polygraph is even less accurate than 80 percent.

Polygraph testing continues to be used for many governmental positions, especially those involving sensitive data or life-and-death responsibility. Applicants for law enforcement jobs, for example, in many locales still take polygraph tests as an important part of the selection process.

INSIGHT 50	*Polygraph testing is now used only in special circumstances owing to its high level of false readings.*

Your Turn

Do you consider polygraph testing an invasion of privacy? Make your argument—pro or con.

_____

_____

_____

_____

_____

_____

HONESTY TESTS

For the vast majority of hiring situations, the successor to the polygraph test is the pencil-and-paper or computer-administered integrity or "honesty" test. Try your hand at several typical questions from such tests:

1. "Have you ever been so entertained by the cleverness of a crook that you hoped he or she would get away with the crime?"
2. "Has a coworker ever shown you how you could cheat your company out of money or products?"
3. "Do you think taking damaged goods from an employer is all right if those goods will otherwise be thrown away?"

4. "Have you ever been involved in any argument with another person that you wished you'd handled differently?"
5. "Have you ever carried a concealed weapon?"
6. "Do you like to hunt?"

A thorough integrity test would typically entail 100 or more such questions. But let's evaluate your results on this short sample.

If you answered "yes" to the first three questions, you'll probably be thanked for your time and shown to the door. In question 1 you were not supposed to find crime entertaining or titillating. In question 2 you were not supposed to hear your coworker out on the topic of cheating. And in question 3 you were not supposed to rationalize the taking of company property based on its condition or future disposition.

But question 4 is an example of a distortion question used to catch applicants who are trying to fool the test. Answering "no" to this question will seem tempting to someone trying to appear extra-good for the purposes of the test; a thoroughly honest person will probably answer "yes," while a dissembler will answer "no."

Questions 5 and 6, although somewhat beyond the range of a typical integrity test, nevertheless are used by some employers to assess an applicant's "fit" with the company. Answering "yes" to these questions will probably not endear an applicant to Saks.

Employers lose billions of dollars each year because they cannot trust their own employees not to steal from them.   **INSIGHT 51**

Your Turn

What has been your own experience with employee dishonesty? Have you observed it in your work situations? What kinds of dishonesty have you observed?

_____

_____

_____

_____

_____

_____

Searching for the Honest Person

Employee dishonesty helps to account for the more than $40 billion lost each year in cash and merchandise to employee theft, according to the Department of Justice. This figure does not include the much larger losses attributable to employee dishonesty with regard to sick days, work habits, and misuse of company property.

To find honest employees, an entire integrity-testing industry has arisen in the last decade. Three companies—London House, Reid Psychological Systems, and Stanton Corporation—now hold 70 percent of that market. On average, an integrity test for one applicant or employee costs the company $10 to $25 per test administration, including scoring and interpretation by the testing service.

What does a failing score indicate? Not merely that an applicant has dishonest impulses, but also that he or she quite probably engages in counterproductive work activities such as purposeful loafing and sabotaging of projects and morale. More than a dozen studies have indicated a strong correlation between people who are dishonest and those who are counterproductive.

Can You Test for Honesty?

In 1991, the American Psychological Association (APA) issued a report on integrity tests, finding that "the preponderance of the evidence" supports the validity of some widely used integrity tests. Since that date, integrity tests have become commonplace in selection procedures. In fact, some organizations have developed their own ways of assessing applicant honesty. In its mini-application, which is published in major newspapers and magazines, the Federal Bureau of Investigation uses a brief but effective honesty check. In addition to asking for such basic information as name, address, and social security number, the application form printed in the advertisement asks this question: "Have you been arrested or convicted for any violation of the law other than minor traffic violations?" Just so there can be no misunderstanding, the question concludes with this parenthetical note: "(Traffic violations other than parking violations are not minor.)"

Candidates willing to sacrifice their honesty for a chance at employment with the FBI will answer "no" to this question, even though their easily accessible traffic record clearly includes speeding tickets or other violations. This relatively small "white lie" gives FBI application reviewers their first (and final) indication that the applicant isn't FBI material.

> *Honesty tests offer a tentative but helpful estimate of the integrity of an applicant before he or she is hired.*
>
> **INSIGHT 52**

Your Turn

Have you taken an honesty test? If so, write your feelings about the test and its use in hiring. If not, write your opinion about the use of honesty tests in the selection process.

_____

_____

_____

_____

_____

_____

PERSONALITY TESTS

Closely allied in nature to honesty tests are a wide range of paper-and-pencil or computer-based instruments intended to describe a potential employee's personality type. Such tests commonly cost between $10 and $100 per administration, and they make up a major product line in the $50 million psychological testing business.

By far the most common personality test is the Myers-Briggs Type Indicator® (MBTI). It sets forth about 100 questions drawn from ordinary life situations. Based on responses to questions, the test scorer can determine the test taker's personality "type." In the Myers-Briggs approach, a person is predisposed to being either extroverted or introverted (E or I), sensing or intuitive (S or N), thinking or feeling (T or F), and perceiving or judging (P or J). Extroverts turn outward in their interests; introverts turn inward. Sensors are fascinated by close details; intuitors seek out the big picture. Thinker's operate locally; feelers operate by emotion. Perceivers look for more and more information; judges want to wrap things up. A person's final test score appears as a series of four letters (e.g., ISTJ) drawn from the types listed previously. This series depicts the person's primary character or habits of mind.

An employee does not "pass" or "fail" such a personality test. Used as a pre-employment instrument, such tests propose to give the company a better idea of how the applicant will fit within a work group or the company culture as a whole, how the applicant will react to different kinds of environments and stresses, and how well the applicant will probably adapt to varying types of job experiences.

In the last decade, hundreds of major corporations (including Allied-Signal, AT&T, Citicorp, Exxon, Honeywell, 3M, and GE) as well as governmental agencies and educational institutions have regularly used the Myers-Briggs instrument for employee development and evaluation. Because the MBTI has not been scientifically validated as a predictor of work success, the Myers-Briggs organization warns employers against making hiring decisions based on MBTI test results.

Do personality tests really work as predictors of work performance? Each test-producing company, of course, has its own story to tell in answer to that question. Probably the safest use of personality tests by companies is to utilize them only for the purposes for which they were intended.

INSIGHT 53	*Although most companies refrain from hiring solely on the basis of personality type (as defined by a personality test), many companies use personality information to develop compatible work teams, make work assignments, and plan employee profiles.*

Your Turn

Have you taken a personality test? If so, what did it reveal about your personality? Do you believe those results to be accurate? If you have not taken a personality test, do you wish to do so? What do you feel you could gain (or not gain) from this testing experience?

_____

_____

_____

_____

_____

SKILLS TESTS

About two-thirds of American companies now use some form of entry skills test as part of the pre-employment process, according to the Bureau of National Affairs. These tests range from general, school-like achievement tests to mechanical aptitude tests to specific quizzes on technical aspects of the prospective job. Common commercial tests include the Flanagan Industrial Test, SRA Mechanical Aptitudes Battery, and Personnel Tests for Industry.

How much freedom does an employer have to test the skills of prospective employees? Prior to *Griggs v. Duke Power* (Supreme Court, 1971), the answer to the question was "plenty!" An employer was free to define "nice to have" characteristics for prospective employees even though these characteristics might be only marginally related to job requirements and job performance. For example, an employer could limit selection consideration only to those applicants without "foreign" accents, or to those applicants who had achieved a B average in school.

In *Griggs v. Duke Power*, the Supreme Court heard the case of an employer who required all employees to have a high school diploma and a passing grade on a standardized intelligence test and a mechanical aptitude test to be considered for promotion. The Court asked whether these requirements were, in fact, job related; that is, were employees who had these qualifications in any verifiable sense better employees than those who did not? Duke Power lacked the evidence to show that its tests and other requirements were predictive of job performance.

Dating from that landmark case, a number of executive orders and amendments to the Civil Rights Act of 1964 have combined to produce an influential set of rules for fair hiring, the Uniform Guidelines. These rubrics help companies determine whether they are acting within legal limits in their hiring practices.

The Uniform Guidelines center on two pillar-like principles:

1. *The principle of validation.* Can an employer demonstrate that tests and other instruments used for employee selection do in fact predict job performance with reasonable accuracy?
2. *The principle of adverse impact.* Even with validated screening devices, are protected groups (as defined by the EEOC) adversely impacted by the use of those measures?

The majority of Americans now belong to some form of protected group as defined by law. As such, they are protected from discrimination of the sorts described throughout this book.   **INSIGHT 54**

Are you a member of a protected group? How would you discover if you are? If you are a member of a protected group, what are your rights? If you are not, can you claim the same rights with regard to fair hiring as those people who are members of protected groups?

DRUG TESTS

Employers bear a crushing economic burden—estimates run as high as $100 billion—owing to drug and alcohol abuse by employees. These costs arise from high turnover, poor work performance, absenteeism, increased medical claims, low morale, theft, and other factors.

The drug-abusing employee is late three times as often as his coworkers, asks for time off twice as often, has two and one-half times as many absences of eight or more days, is five times more likely to file a workers' compensation claim, and is involved in accidents more than three times as often.

Typical on-the-job symptoms of drug abuse are inability to pay attention, difficulty with simple arithmetic, prolonged trips to the rest room, frequent absenteeism, poor personal hygiene, lapses in memory, and inattention to detail.

Given the social gravity and bottom-line expense of the drug problem, it is understandable that most American companies now screen for drug abuse during the pre-employment process. In most cases, this testing takes place as an ordinary and relatively inexpensive part of the pre-employment physical.

The Accuracy of Drug Testing

Urine analysis remains the most common method of drug testing at present, in large part because of its low cost ($15–$25), noninvasive administration, and ease of use with large groups. Since the 1990s, however, the relative inaccuracy of urine analysis has been recognized by the medical community. The Centers for Disease Control (CDC) and the National Institute on Drug Abuse (NIDA) have independently conducted a series of evaluations to measure the accuracy of drug testing by companies. In one such evaluation, the drug detection error rate averaged 30 percent among laboratories used by the companies.

What goes wrong in such testing? CDC researchers point to carelessness in laboratories, untrained employees, inadequate testing equipment, and cross-reactivity errors (such as when common over-the-counter drugs such as Contac, Sudafed, and decongestants register falsely as amphetamines; cough syrups as opiates; antibiotics as cocaine; and Datril, Advil, and Nuprin as marijuana—even certain types of herbal tea can produce false positives for illegal drugs). These sources of testing errors only multiply when employers try to conduct their own on-site testing using do-it-yourself drug-screening kits.

No matter what the origin of the error, real people and their employment opportunities are frequently devastated by the stigmas of failing a drug test. Given the relative inaccuracy of urine analysis for drug testing, it is hardly surprising that applicants and employees often resent potentially stigmatizing drug tests. In response, companies using urine analysis as their primary check for drugs are increasingly making available a more expensive ($75–$150) gas chromatography–mass spectrometry test to confirm an initial failure in drug screening. In some states, applicants have the right to insist on this additional test.

Drug testing is legal in most states and for most hiring circumstances. Applicants should seek backup testing if their results are inaccurate.	**INSIGHT 55**

Your Turn

Have you been tested for drugs as part of an employment application? If so, write about your feelings about the experience (you need not reveal your results). If not, write about whether you feel drug testing is necessary and advisable for most jobs.

_____

_____

_____

_____

_____

COMPUTER-ASSISTED INTERVIEWS

The idea of a computer posing questions on-screen to a job applicant may seem the stuff of science fiction. But especially for entry-level positions, many major companies, including Macy's, Lockheed Martin, and Marriott Corporation, use computer-delivered interviews. Interestingly, applicants seem to respond more honestly to questions posed by the computer than they do to the same questions posed by a human interviewer. In one study, students revealed grade-point averages and SAT scores more accurately to the computer than to a human interviewer. A Duke University study found that people would admit to an alcohol problem more honestly to a computer. And *Personnel Journal* states that

> several corporate users [of computer interviewing systems] report that applicants display similar candor with the computer, even with questions about theft, drug abuse, and likeliness to quit. For example, an interviewer in the retail industry says that when his company computer asks applicants how long they plan to work for the firm, approximately 15 percent reply "less than a year." The firm is able to make a significant reduction in turnover by the response to a single question.

Imagine the hours, money, and personal energy saved by scheduling a long line of applicants for a few minutes each at a computer station instead of in an interview room with a human interviewer. At the computer, the applicant would be asked a series of multiple-choice questions. For example:

1. Are you applying to work part-time or full-time?
   a. part-time (fewer than 40 hours)
   b. full-time (40 hours per week)
   c. whatever is available
2. The position for which you are applying may require you to lift boxes that weigh 25 to 30 pounds. Will this be a problem for you?
   a. It will definitely be a problem.
   b. It might be a problem.
   c. It will not be a problem.
3. Have you ever had a job where you worked directly with customers?
   a. yes
   b. no

   If yes . . .
4. How would your supervisor at that job rate your customer-service skills?
   a. outstanding
   b. above average
   c. average
   d. below average
   e. I don't know

Remember that applicants will tend to answer such questions more honestly for the computer than for a human interviewer. Perhaps applicants may feel that the computer somehow "knows" the correct answer, and they want to avoid being caught in a lie. Or interviewees may be responding to the fact that the computer does not judge them or show disappointment or confusion at their answers. Any response is equally acceptable to the computer.

Virtually all computer-assisted interview programs print out a scorecard of sorts for review by personnel officers and managers. These human evaluators can see at a glance how the applicants responded to questions and, for once, can compare apples with apples—since identical questions were asked of each applicant.

More sophisticated interview programs can give hiring decision makers even more valuable data, including

- *latency of response information*—how long the interviewee paused before answering certain questions,

- *change-of-mind responses*—in which the interviewee canceled one answer in favor of another, and

- *contradictory responses*—in which applicants answered similar or related questions in contradictory ways. (For example, a candidate may say "yes" to "Do you smoke at work?" and, later in the computer interview, also say "yes" to "Do you now work in a no-smoking environment?"

The typical computer-assisted interview process presents 50 to 75 questions on-screen to the applicant. The half hour or so it takes for the applicant to respond is significantly less than the time such questions and answers might take in a face-to-face interview. And, unlike the poor note taking practiced by many human interviewers, the computer keeps secure, organized, accurate, and accessible records. But perhaps the greatest advantage of the computer-assisted interview is that it is "blind" to the factors that bias the interviewer for or against the applicant: age, gender, race, height, weight, relative attractiveness, scent, clothing, accent, and so forth. Although these factors may play a role in later in-person stages of the hiring process, at least the "first cut" of applicants is made without such influence, thanks to the computer.

Computers now provide a cost-effective way to deliver baseline questions to applicants and accurately store their results.

INSIGHT 56

Your Turn

Would you prefer to be interviewed by a computer or a human being at your initial interview for an entry-level position? Explain your response.

_____

_____

_____

_____

_____

_____

Summing Up

Employers continue to seek corroborating information to support the claims of applicants with regard to their abilities, knowledge, skills, and experiences. In general, courts have permitted such testing so long as it treats all groups fairly and is directly related to job requirements. Testing that risks a high degree of error puts both companies and applicants in jeopardy and must be addressed by backup testing that ensures accuracy.

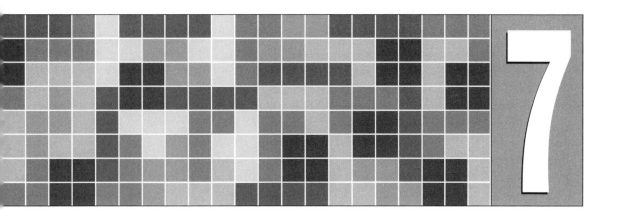

The Selection Interview, Performance Appraisal Interview, and Exit Interview

GOALS

- Summarize the main features of the selection interview.
- Understand the purposes and techniques of the performance appraisal interview.
- Grasp the main features and methods of the exit interview.

THE SELECTION INTERVIEW

By far the most common type of interview in American business, the selection interview places those who know the company best in direct contact with those who want to join the company. The selection interview has traditionally been one-on-one, for periods ranging from 15 minutes to an hour or more. In the last decade, more companies are using group interview, with several interviewers to one applicant, as a way of speeding up and giving more validity to the interview process. As the interviewee in any of the following situations, you can prepare to do your best by understanding what the interviewer is trying to accomplish—and the mistakes that interviewers sometimes make.

Purposes of the Selection Interview

- To collect data, through questioning and discussion, that can be used to choose the best employees available. Such data include evidence of the candidate's intelligence, aptitude, attitudes, personality, habits, activities, interests, education, background, work history, integrity, communication skills, and personal/professional goals.
- To communicate important information about the company to the candidate.

Common Problems

1. *Interviewers talk too much.* Applicants, because they are the primary source for decision making, should do approximately 80 percent of the talking during the interview.
2. *Interviewers ask the wrong questions.* Many applicants come prepared with "conned" answers regarding their education, career goals, work history, and so forth. Interviewers must ask questions (such as those that follow) that test the applicant's ability to think quickly, express clearly, and get to the point.
3. *Applicants mumble and stumble owing to nerves.* Often the brightest applicants suffer most from nervous tension, perhaps because they are so motivated to perform well. At the beginning of the interview, skilled interviewers take a few minutes of their interview time to put the candidate at ease through small talk.
4. *Interviewers do not record data for later decision making.* For legal reasons and effective selection procedures, interviewers must take notes on what the applicant said, how he or she appeared, and how well he or she communicated.

Sample Questions

1. Please tell me about your previous job.
2. What do you believe were your major responsibilities in that position?
3. What kind of job experiences have you had that relate to the position you seek?
4. What aspects of your previous job did you like?
5. What aspects of your previous job did you dislike?
6. What are some of the things you spent the most time doing in your previous job? How much time did you spend on each?
7. What are some of the assignments in your previous job that you found difficult to do? Why?
8. What are some of the assignments in your previous job that you did particularly well? Why?
9. Tell me about a problem you solved on your previous job.
10. What did you do when you couldn't solve a problem in your previous job?
11. Describe your boss's method of management. How did you respond to that management style?
12. For what things did your boss compliment you?
13. In your previous job, how much work was done on your own? As part of a team?
14. What was the most innovative idea you introduced in your previous job?
15. Describe your techniques for getting the job done.

Personal Background, Attitudes, and Goals

1. What schooling have you had that can be helpful in performing this job?
2. What are your own objectives with regard to this position?
3. What are your long-term career objectives?
4. In your career, where do you want to be in one (three, five) year(s) from now?
5. What do you plan to do to reach your career objectives?
6. How do you feel about the progress you've made so far in your present or previous job?
7. Do you believe your talents and abilities are well matched for this job? How and why?

8. What are your greatest assets?

9. How did you choose the school you attended?

10. Did you change your course of study? Why?

11. Did you change schools? Why?

12. Why did you major in your particular field?

13. In what extracurricular activities were you involved in school?

14. What made you choose those particular activities?

15. What accomplishments did you feel proud of at school?

16. What experiences at school do you wish you had a chance to do over? Why?

17. How did you pay for your education?

18. Did you hold any leadership positions at school?

19. What things interest you outside of work?

20. What do you like to do best?

21. What things give you the greatest satisfaction?

22. Have your interests changed in recent years?

23. How well did you do in school?

24. What grades did you receive?

25. In what courses did you do best?

26. With what courses did you have the most trouble?

27. From what courses did you get the most benefit? Why?

28. From what courses did you get the least benefit? Why?

29. Do you feel your grades fairly reflect your ability? Why or why not?

30. If you had it to do over again, would you take the same course of study? Why or why not?

31. How do you view the job for which you are now applying?

32. If you were to obtain this job, in what areas could you contribute immediately? Where would you need training?

33. What barriers do you see that might prevent you from performing your job as effectively as you would like to?

34. Do you have the tools and support that you need to do your job?

35. What do you understand to be the mission or purpose of this company?

36. How do you feel about the day-to-day, routine tasks involved with this position?

37. How well do you work under pressure? Give some examples.

38. How well do you get along with your peers?

39. What kind of people rub you the wrong way?

40. How do you go about motivating other people?
41. What kinds of problems do you enjoy solving?
42. What can you tell me about your level of ambition?
43. How do you spend your free time?
44. What newspapers and magazines do you read regularly?
45. What is your definition of success?
46. What did you learn from your previous position?
47. What can you tell me about your level of creativity?
48. Do you work better alone or as part of a team? Explain.
49. What motivates you?
50. Why should this company hire you?

No interviewer has time to ask all the questions she wishes of an applicant. A selection of questions must be made on the basis of their relevance to job requirements.   **INSIGHT 57**

Your Turn

From the list of questions just given, choose five that you feel are particularly important for see-ing deeply into the potential of a job applicant. For each question, explain why you chose it.

_____

_____

_____

_____

_____

_____

ORGANIZE YOUR THOUGHTS FOR SUCCESSFUL INTERVIEW RESPONSES

This book does not advise "canned" answers to typical interview questions. Although a candidate should think through what he might say in response to the kinds of selection questions listed in this chapter, any attempt to memorize mini-speeches to use during interviews will surely backfire. Interviewers are quick to spot the candidate who is spouting preformed answers instead of responding spontaneously and authentically to interview questions.

However, a job candidate can and should practice "placing" parts of an interview answer advantageously. The following five strategies can convert a wandering, confusing interview response into a succinct, compelling answer:

1. *Headline your main point.* In the same way that a newspaper or magazine provides a headline that sums up the thrust of the accompanying story, so a job candidate should begin an answer by getting right to the point. After all, the interviewee doesn't know in advance when or whether the interviewer will cut in with another question. Too many candidates have been left thinking "Wait, I haven't gotten to my point yet" when the interviewer interrupts a response to move on with the interview.

2. *Place support material after the main point, not before it.* Job seekers often make the mistake of telling about the details before they let the interviewer know what these specifics are intended to show. The unfortunate effect is similar to naming random numbers—1, 4, 3, 5, 2, 6, 9—before revealing that they add up to 30. An interviewer can't make sense out of supporting details until she knows what they are supposed to prove or illustrate.

3. *Tell how many parts your answer has before listing those parts.* Let's say, for example, you have three reasons for wanting to work for the company. Begin your answer by telling the interviewer that you have three reasons, then explain them. If you do not reveal how many parts your answer has, the interviewer may cut in before you have completed your response. In addition, your answer will seem disorganized if its parts are linked only by words such as "and," "also," and "another." It's much better to say up front that you have three reasons, then use "First," "Second," and "Third" or "Finally" to begin your explanation of each of your reasons.

4. *In multipart responses, put your most important answer first in the list.* Even when you have begun by telling the interviewer that your answer has three parts, you have no guarantee that the interviewer will be patient enough to hear all three parts. An interviewer may cut in to move the interview along or may interrupt with a probe or question that turns conversation in a different direction and prevents you from completing your intended three-part response. Therefore, put your best foot forward in any multipart answer.

5. *For longer answers (in excess of 20 seconds or so) provide a succinct "so what" wrap-up at the end of your response.* A longer interview response should not wind down to a few unimportant last words. The interviewer (like any

listener) will pay particular attention to the first portion of your response and the end of the response. Make sure that your final words provide a memorable point or "cap" to your extended answer.

THE PERFORMANCE APPRAISAL INTERVIEW

Performance appraisals are often conducted informally, as when a group of managers meets to discuss the performance of their employees. Or performance appraisals can be formal, with set dates, cycles, and written appraisal instruments. In either case, the results of performance appraisals affect what matters most to employees: promotions, pay increases, relative power in the organization, transfers, and even terminations. Not surprisingly, the actions of employers in these areas have been rather thoroughly limited by federal and state laws.

The import of these laws, as contained in the Uniform Guidelines for Employee Selection Procedures (U.S. Government Printing Office, 1978) is as follows:

1. Make sure the criteria by which you are evaluating employees are in fact important to successful performance of the job. If the ability to write well, for example, does not affect job performance, it should not be used as an evaluation criterion.

2. Build those criteria directly into a rating instrument so that your judgments are based upon success factors, not arbitrary opinion.

3. Take care to communicate your standards for performance to employees. This communication should be written as well as oral. Employers are wise to devise a "sign-off" procedure to demonstrate that employees have read and understood the performance standards.

4. Train all evaluators, including supervisors and managers, in the use of any instruments or feedback forms used for evaluation. These instructions should be written and training procedures should be thorough enough to produce competent evaluators. The employer should be able to demonstrate a means of quality review and quality control of the evaluation process.

5. Document all evaluations, including your reasons for action taken. When challenged in Court, employers usually must produce written evidence showing the basis on which the employee was evaluated and the method by which results were determined.

6. Oversee the evaluation process, making sure that changing job conditions are reflected in accompanying changes in the evaluation process.

Common Problems

1. *Employees perceive questions as disciplinary in nature.* Especially when questions involve task performance, superior–subordinate relations, or time allocation, employees often feel that they are being criticized rather than evaluated. As a result, their answers are defensive and often somewhat hostile. Interviewers must make clear that, far from imposing criticism, they want to know the employee's thoughts and feelings about work situations.

2. *Employees look upon the process as unfair.* Because they do not know or have not been informed of the standards by which they are being evaluated, employees often think of performance appraisals as "personality contests" or opportunities to flatter the boss. Going in to the performance appraisal, the employee should know (a) what will be discussed, (b) why those topics matter for job performance, and (c) what will be done with the information given in the interview.

3. *Interviewers fail to refer to specific facts and to ask specific questions.* In such an interview environment, employees can come to feel a free-floating sense of guilt and dread, somewhat akin to "Original Sin." The interviewer hints that "something" isn't quite right but never puts a finger on the precise project, report, or manager at issue. As a consequence, the employee cannot respond specifically and factually.

4. *Interviewers convey dislike or disapproval for the employee, not the employee's behavior.* If interviewers want to understand and evaluate the actions of employees, they must keep the focus of the interview steadily on those actions instead of on more diffuse topics such as personality. Employees can often provide meaningful explanations of particular actions they took. It's almost impossible, by contrast, to explain why they are who they are.

Sample Questions

1. What do you understand the purpose or mission of your department to be?
2. Tell me how well you think your department is structured to accomplish its mission effectively.
3. Tell me how you allocate your time among the various tasks you do each day.
4. How well are you able to use your skills and abilities in your present job?
5. How would you characterize the contribution you're now making to your department?

6. Are there any functions you are now performing that could be reduced or eliminated?

7. What input do you have into the way decisions are made in your department?

8. How do you feel about your opportunities for growth and development on the job?

9. Do you know how well you are performing in your job? How do you know?

10. Do you know what is expected of you on the job? How do you know?

11. What kind of recognition do you get for the work you do? From whom?

12. What are your aspirations for the future?

13. Do you feel that work is allocated properly in your department?

14. Are there any circumstances that keep you from performing your job the way you would like?

15. In the past year (six months, month, etc.) what accomplishment could you point to as an example of your skill and expertise?

16. Tell me about a project or task that didn't go entirely as you wished. What were the problems? How did you try to solve them?

17. Tell me about a coworker who appeared to interfere with your progress on the job.

18. Do you work best alone or as a member of a team? Why?

19. If we added employees to your group, describe the kind of person we should hire.

20. How are you like or unlike that person?

21. What things seem to be changing about the way you do your job or about your work situation here? How do you feel about those changes?

22. How do you feel about the way you are managed?

23. How do you manage your subordinates?

24. How would you characterize your relations with fellow employees?

25. How do you know when you've done a good job?

26. What would you like to change most about your work situation?

A performance appraisal interview aims primarily at helping the employee recognize what he or she does well on the job as well as what can be improved.   **INSIGHT 58**

Your Turn

Tell about performance appraisals you have received in work- or school-related environments. What did you find helpful in these appraisals? What could have been more helpful?

THE EXIT INTERVIEW

Approximately 40 percent of American corporations, large and small, conduct exit interviews as a regular part of the personnel process. An exit interview is a nondefensive, nonjudgmental conversation with employees leaving the company. Ideally, the interview is conducted by someone other than the employee's direct supervisor or a superior who will later be used as a reference.

Purposes of the Exit Interview

- To learn the exiting employee's perceptions of strengths and weaknesses within the company, including attitudes toward salary, benefits, supervision, work assignments, company leadership, and work conditions.
- To understand why the employee is attracted to other companies, perhaps competitors.
- To establish or maintain favorable relations between the company and exiting employees, many of whom will return to the company at a later date, establish a venture with the company at some point in time, and/or will make recommendations to friends about employment there.

Common Problems

1. *The exiting employee is interviewed by his or her immediate supervisor or a superior who will later be used as a job reference.* In the first case, the employee may be unable to discuss the real problems on the job—especially when those problems directly involved the personality, management style, or intelligence of the supervisor. In the second case, the employee may hold back frank opinions for fear of alienating a superior who may later act as a recommender.

2. *Topics are phrased in a threatening, punitive, or judgmental way.* It does little good to ask an employee, "What could you have done to make your stay here more successful?" The exiting employee, after all, has little motivation to answer such questions—he or she is leaving. Questions must be phrased (as in the following examples) so that the employee is made to feel like a helpful consultant to the company, not a naughty child.

3. *Questions are not open enough to let the exiting employee have his or her say.* Too often, exit interviewers assume that they know why employees are leaving. Favorite reasons are salary, workload, or better opportunities. Interviewers have a tendency, in such cases, to limit discussion entirely to those topics. As a result, exiting employees may not get a chance to explain their real feelings with regard to their work experience.

4. *The interviewer fails to explain what use will be made of the opinions given by the employee.* Ideally, all exit interview data should be treated anonymously. If an exiting employee gives supervisors or coworkers negative evaluations, she should not have to worry about being "blackballed" in the profession by those people. To create a climate in which the exiting employee will speak freely, the interviewer must explicitly assure anonymity and confidentiality regarding recording and using the opinions given. The following is a sample assurance statement:

> Bob, we appreciate this chance to get your thoughts and feelings about the company. Everything we discuss in the next half hour will be confidential and anonymous. You're not being recorded. The only notes I'm making are for our statistical use in determining where the company is doing well and where it needs to improve. Your name will not be attached to any opinions you give.

Sample Questions

1. Tell me about your salary history with the company.
2. How fairly were you treated with regard to salary by the company?
3. How often and on what basis was your performance evaluated?
4. How fair was the evaluation in your opinion?
5. Share with me your attitudes about the benefits package at the company.
6. Which benefits mattered to you most? Which mattered least?
7. How did you feel about your physical working conditions at the company?
8. How did you feel about your social working conditions, including your coworkers and supervisor?
9. How appropriate was your workload, given your skills and level of experience? Did you have enough to do? Too much? Too little?

10. Within your work group, how fairly was work distributed, in your opinion?

11. What is your attitude toward your climb up the ladder during your time with the company? Did you make the progress you wished? If not, what do you think were the barriers?

12. Tell me about any barriers that you felt were holding you back from achieving your goals with the company.

13. How would you describe your own feelings or morale toward your job? Toward the company?

14. What seemed to be the feelings or morale of others you worked with toward their jobs? Toward the company?

15. In your opinion how could the company improve morale among the workforce?

16. Tell me about your relations with coworkers.

17. Tell me about your relations with your supervisor.

18. Tell me about your relations with your subordinates.

19. What changes would you recommend to improve operations in your work unit? In the company?

20. In your opinion, what would make this company more competitive?

21. What company policies or procedures did you dislike? Why?

22. In looking for employment elsewhere, what were the primary factors that attracted you to another position?

23. What aspects of this job will you be glad to leave behind?

24. What advice would you have for senior management here?

25. What other topics do you feel we should discuss? (Or what other topics would you ask an exiting employee to discuss?)

INSIGHT 59   *Employees leaving the company often have valuable insight into how the company can improve.*

Your Turn

Imagine that you are in charge of exit interviews for a company. How would you go about motivating exiting employees to speak candidly with you about their experiences with the company?

_____

_____

Summing Up

Selection, performance appraisal, and exit interviews require the same interviewing skills as those taught in earlier chapters. The suggested questions for each interview type can be altered as necessary to produce a battery of questions that suit the individual and the company.

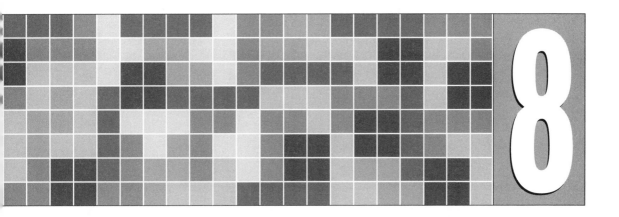

The Counseling Interview, Information Interview, and Negotiation Interview

8

GOALS

- Recognize the counseling interview as an opportunity to understand and deal with potential problems before they rise to conflict levels.

- Grasp the importance of the information interview as a way to solicit and manage knowledge that resides in human heads rather than file drawers or disk storage.

- Focus on the potential of the negotiation interview as a way of achieving a "win–win" conclusion for the parties involved.

THE COUNSELING INTERVIEW

The purpose of this interview is twofold: to uncover career-related personal or interpersonal problems and to guide the interviewee toward a resolution of those problems. Though all counseling deals to some degree with psychological issues, the following discussion focuses on the counseling interview in a business environment, not in a medical or psychotherapeutic context.

Purposes of the Counseling Interview

- To create an atmosphere of trust in which deep-seated and potentially threatening topics or attitudes can be discussed.
- To understand topics and problems discussed from the interviewee's point of view.
- To lead the interviewee to courses of thought and action that will prove personally and professionally beneficial. (The interviewer achieves this goal primarily through active listening, empathy, and information sharing.)

Common Problems

1. *The interviewee feels that his or her opinions don't matter.* The counseling interview cannot succeed if it is viewed (by interviewer or interviewee) as a lecture session. Though the interviewer often has company-approved ends in mind for the interview, those goals should not be imposed in such a way as to squelch expression of feelings or exploration of alternatives.

2. *The interviewee doesn't trust the interviewer.* Truly volatile personal or interpersonal issues are difficult to discuss with even close friends, much less a counselor in the workplace. Inevitably a certain degree of highly personal information—marriage, self-image, health fears, and so forth—come up during the counseling interview. The interviewer must therefore be explicit in assuring the interviewee that the session is confidential. For this reason, companies have had little luck in asking supervisors and managers to double as counseling interviewers. They are usually too involved in the politics and power of the work environment to be "trustable" by those counseled. Instead, companies employ professionally trained counselors to handle these interviews.

3. *The interviewer is powerless within the organization to do anything about the dilemmas discussed by the interviewee.* When an interviewee spills his deepest thoughts and feelings about a work situation, it's not enough for the interviewer to say, in effect, "Well, do the best you can"—thereby putting the burden for change entirely on the interviewee. Counseling interviewers should have direct communication, with necessary clout, with all levels of management in the company. The goal, after all, is to resolve problems, not merely share them.

Sample Assurance of Confidentiality

Linda, we're here to discuss the obvious problems that have been occurring between you and Ms. Johnson, your supervisor. Before we begin, I want you to know that anything you tell me will be handled confidentially. I won't report anything you say to Ms. Johnson or anyone else without your permission.

Sample Statement of Purpose

Mike, we're meeting to see if we can get to the root of the morale problem among your employees. I'm not interested in placing blame—I just want to understand how you view the situation and to see if together we can find a solution.

Sample Questions

(If a particular situation is at issue, substitute it wherever "the problem" is mentioned in the following statements.)

1. What do you think we should talk about?
2. How do you feel about this discussion? Do you think it can help?
3. What could we do in the next half hour (hour, etc.) to get to the heart of the matter?
4. Tell me about some of the personalities involved in the problem.
5. Tell me specifically what others do that upsets you. Describe your feelings as completely as you can.
6. I can understand your feelings of frustration and anger. Tell me how you express those feelings.
7. Things obviously aren't the way you would wish them to be. Describe for me how things should be.
8. Start from the beginning and tell me how the problem developed.
9. What do you think your supervisor (coworker, etc.) expects of you?
10. How do you feel about those expectations?
11. In what ways should you have been treated differently by others?
12. If you had complete control over this situation, what would you do?
13. This may be difficult, but I'd like you to try to describe the problem from the other person's point of view.
14. In most problems, there are spectators and participants. In this problem, who are the spectators—people on the sidelines watching the struggle? Who are the participants battling it out on the field?

15. Do you leave these feelings at work each day or take them home with you?

16. Give me a worst-case scenario for this problem. How bad can it get? What will you do then?

17. What do you think caused the problem?

18. With whom do you share your feelings about this problem? What do they say?

19. You said there were good days and bad days regarding this problem. Tell me what makes a good day. What makes a bad day?

20. Once I completely understand your point of view, what do you think I should do?

21. I'm going to say back to you a few of the key words you've used to describe the problem. For each word, tell me what thoughts or feelings you have. (Proceed to say back key words—e.g., hostility, insubordination, attitude problem, smart aleck.)

22. This problem has kept you from doing some other things you wish to do. What are some of those things?

23. If (name a party to the problem) were sitting here with us, what would you say to this person?

24. Let's reverse roles. Ask me the questions that matter most in this problem.

25. As you look at the problem, what aspects are within your own power to solve? What aspects are out of your power?

INSIGHT 60   *In a business context, the counseling interview must stop short of psychotherapy, but still must elicit deep feelings that help to interpret an employee's actions.*

Your Turn

Imagine that a friend of yours was asked to visit a company counselor to discuss attitudes and behaviors toward the opposite gender. In what ways do you think this discussion should be different from a discussion on the same topic held with your friend's boss?

_____

_____

_____

THE INFORMATION INTERVIEW

An information interview seeks to gather facts and sources for facts. It is typically used by a new manager getting "up to speed" on projects within the work unit; by media specialists within the company, gathering information for press releases, advertising, and training materials; and by financial personnel seeking data for budgeting and decision making.

Purposes of the Information Interview

- To collect facts in an organized way for later use in planning, publications, training, or decision making.
- To determine sources for facts, including the relative authority and trustworthiness of those sources.

Common Problems

1. *Interviewees hold back information.* Interviewers must explain their "need to know" with care and patience to encourage a free flow of information from interviewees. Knowledge in organizations, after all, is a form of power: What the boss knows can hurt you.

2. *Interviewers ask for facts in a disorganized manner.* The "shotgun" approach to information seeking discourages full disclosure on the part of interviewees. Like a vein of ore, one line of questioning should be thoroughly explored before turning to another line. A technical question about wing stability, for example, should not be followed immediately by a question on overall funding for research and development. Interviewees will conclude that the interviewer doesn't know what he is asking or that the interviewer doesn't understand the significance of the answers received.

3. *Interviewers fail to record facts in a visible way.* Especially where technical explanations and complicated descriptions are concerned, interviewees need to know that their words are being recorded accurately. Too often interviewers simply nod "uh-huh" after an exhaustive rehearsal of facts by the interviewee. If no recording method (tape, notes, etc.) is present, the interviewee will tend to give more and more brief, simplistic answers.

Sample Statement of Purpose

In the next hour I'm going to ask you for information regarding the simple B-17 project. What you tell me is being recorded so that we can make a printed transcript. You'll have a chance to review the transcript and to make any changes before we use your information to plan training manuals.

Sample Questions

(Substitute "this situation," "this proposal," "this product," or another phrase as appropriate for "this project.")

1. Tell me about the development of this project.
2. Tell me about the people involved in this project.
3. If the development of this project could be divided into stages, what would they be?
4. Tell me about the most difficult aspects of this project.
5. Tell me about how the client has responded to this project.
6. How would you describe this project to a 10-year-old?
7. How does this project differ from _____. (fill in another project)
8. What financial information is available on this project?
9. What risks does the company face in backing this project?
10. What risks do employees face in working on the project?
11. How will the project look to us in two (three, five) years?
12. How is the project like other projects completed by the company? How is it different?
13. What basic facts should I know about the materials used in the project?
14. What are the costs, including projected future costs of those materials?
15. How is the project managed? By whom?
16. What are the milestones for project completion and implementation? How were those milestones determined?
17. How will we measure the relative success of the project?
18. What is the essential value of the project? (to the company, to society, etc.)
19. What is the reputation of the project? (in the profession, in the company, among the public, etc.)
20. Who are the most knowledgeable about the project?
21. How is the development of the project being recorded or tracked?
22. On what technologies does the success of the project depend?
23. On what social attitudes does the success of the project depend?
24. What will motivate end users to buy, participate in, sponsor, or fund the project?
25. What aspects of the project must be considered proprietary?

> *An information interview succeeds to the extent that it avoids other agendas, such as salesmanship or negotiation.*   **INSIGHT 61**

Your Turn

If you have conducted an information interview, tell how it went. If not, write about a potential information interview that could help you with some aspect of your work or school life, including your career plans.

_____

_____

_____

_____

_____

_____

_____

THE NEGOTIATION INTERVIEW

In the negotiation interview, parties with opposed interests and points of view join in an effort to reach a mutually agreeable compromise. Negotiation interviews are common in labor/management situations, vendor/purchaser price conferences, contract discussions, requests for raises or positions, and so forth.

Purposes of the Negotiation Interview

- To maximize what is in the interest of both parties while minimizing what is not in the interest of either party or only one party.
- To build understanding and relations conducive to working among parties.

Common Problems

1. *Negotiators can be blinded by ego.* Particularly in heated negotiation interviews, participants can be heard to grumble, "You can't do that to

me." They have so deeply internalized their mission that an objection to an idea or proposal becomes an objection to them personally. Negotiators must learn, through training and experience, not to take heated objections personally.

2. *Negotiators quit talking.* The game of negotiation involves "tough stands," "final offers," and "absolute courses of action" that are far from tough, final, or absolute. Both sides to the negotiation bluster and bluff as a way of determining just how much the opponent is willing to give. Negotiations fail, therefore, when negotiators end discussion as soon as such bluffs occur. A continuing dialogue can often reach compromises that seemed impossible at earlier stages of negotiation.

3. *Negotiators go back on their word.* Progress in negotiations usually happens verbally—one side is willing to go on to certain compromises based on verbal concessions made by the other side. Trust and the possibility for compromise break down, however, when one side "forgets" or goes back on its verbal assurances. To prevent such backtracking, all major points in the negotiation process should be set down in writing, then signed off by participants. While such a sign-off procedure usually does not have the true contractual status, it does help to avoid the "but you said; no we didn't" problem in verbal negotiation.

Sample Statement of Purpose

We're all here because there are substantial profits to be made on all sides by a mutually agreeable contract. We have different attitudes toward what that contract should contain. But in the coming hours and days, we should not lose track of our goal: finding terms to give us all a strong incentive to sign the final contract.

Sample Questions

1. What portion of our proposal can you agree with?
2. With what specific aspects of our proposal do you disagree? Why?
3. What counterproposal can you offer?
4. What do our proposals have in common? How do they differ?
5. Of the items with which you disagree, which matter to you the most? Which least?
6. In what areas do you think compromise is most easily reached?
7. In difficult areas of compromise, what trade-offs are possible?

8. What historical (social, political, etc.) reasons help to explain your stand on _____. (some aspect of their proposal)

9. What do you want to understand more about in our proposal?

10. How would our proposal, if agreed upon, affect your people?

11. What do we have to lose if we fail to reach an agreement? What do we have to gain if we succeed?

12. How much time can pass before any agreement becomes impossible or irrelevant?

13. What do you think should be included in an ideal compromise?

14. What are your primary goals in this agreement? What goals are secondary?

15. What are your greatest concerns with this agreement as it now stands?

16. What do your people expect from you when you come out of this negotiation?

17. What do your superiors expect from you when you come out of this negotiation?

18. What kind of time frame should we be working within to reach an agreement?

19. What issues can we discuss on an individual basis? Can we separate them out for agreement prior to reaching an agreement on the overall proposal?

20. Of the points we've agreed to discuss, what priority should we follow?

21. What incentive would you require to agree with certain aspects of our proposal?

22. How much consultation with your people will be required for you to go forward on points of agreement?

23. Can we reach a final agreement by setting aside issues on which we disagree for later discussion?

24. Would a break be helpful as a period during which to consider certain points?

25. Now that we've reached a compromise, what is the best way to announce and implement our agreement?

The negotiation interview begins by careful listening to the positions of the interested parties. All parties must be involved in this listening process if the negotiation is to succeed.	**INSIGHT 62**

Your Turn

What was the last thing you negotiated? How did you approach the negotiation process? Did you feel you won, lost, or tied? How could the negotiation process have been improved from your point of view?

_____

_____

_____

_____

_____

_____

Summing Up

The counseling, information, and negotiation forms of interviewing all require special sensitivity on the part of the interviewer. Pressing the interviewee too hard in any of these interview types can backfire. In the counseling interview, an interviewee may "clam up" in response to overly intrusive or badgering questions. The interviewee in an information interview may retreat to general, "safe" statements if the interviewer has not conveyed a legitimate "need to know" for his or her questions. Finally, in the negotiation interview, both parties may withdraw from the process unless there is a clear understanding that the negotiation interview is intended to explore options, not to pit egos against one another.

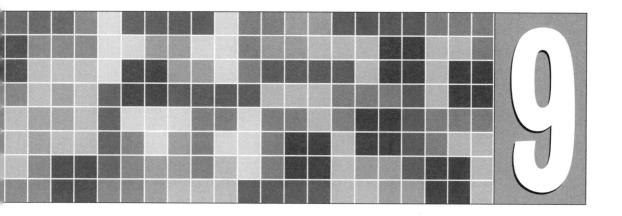

The Persuasion/Sales Interview and Disciplinary Interview

GOALS

- Come to know the persuasion/sales interview as an opportunity for conveying information and stimulating action.

- Understand the disciplinary interview as an opportunity to define and deal with behaviors that stand in the way of an employee's success.

THE PERSUASION/SALES INTERVIEW

This common interview occurs whenever one party tries to guide another toward a desired course of thinking or action through questions and discussion. Among the many types of persuasion/sales interviews are the transfer/new responsibilities interview, in which a manager tries to persuade a subordinate to willingly take another position or new responsibilities in the company; the resources interview, in which a manager apportions or seeks funding; and the client interview, in which the salesperson determines the client's needs and how they can be met.

Purposes of the Persuasion/Sales Interview

- To convince the interviewee of the desirability of a course of action or thinking.
- To overcome objections to that course of action or thinking.
- To build ongoing interpersonal relationships conducive to problem solving.

Common Problems

1. *The interviewer knows the answer but the interviewee doesn't know the question.* Some persuaders, caught up in the enthusiasm of their project and "pitch," forget to solicit the interviewee's needs and attitudes. Even the most polished persuasional or sales approach will fall on deaf ears under these circumstances.

2. *The interviewee is asked too soon for a decision.* Particularly in complex matters such as new job responsibilities or financial decisions, interviewees need time to come to terms with new ideas.

3. *The interviewee doesn't have a chance to ask questions.* Many people in sales are by nature both assertive and controlling. They like to take a stand, overcome objections, and come out the winner. As positive as these qualities are for success in sales, they must not smother the interviewee's chance to ask questions. "I know what you are thinking," goes the typical sales pitch. But interviewees appreciate a less presumptuous approach—one that sincerely asks what they're thinking.

Sample Questions

(Substitute "process," "person," "promotion," or "policy" in place of "product" as appropriate.)

1. In trying to achieve your goals, what product have you tried?
2. How did that product work out?
3. What would you have changed in that product?
4. What did your people have to say about the product?
5. If you had continued to use the product, what would have been the result?

6. What contact did you have with those who made the product? What was your feeling about that contact?

7. What kind of product do you need?

8. What other needs may develop for you in the future?

9. How would you like to interface with the supplier of the product?

10. What should the product do for you?

11. What should the product not do?

12. How much do you wish to pay for the product?

13. How much would you be willing to pay for a product that met your needs entirely?

14. How much product will you require?

15. By what process will you determine which product to buy?

16. How will you decide how well you like the product?

17. Who in your company will be in charge of using the product?

18. What experience or background do you require for those using the product?

19. Where will the product be used?

20. What are your short-term and long-term business goals?

21. How can we assist you in reaching those goals?

22. When will you decide which product to buy?

23. What interests you about our product?

24. What concerns you most about the purchase or use of our product?

25. What questions do you have about our product or service?

The persuasion/sales interview focuses first on what the client needs, not what the salesperson has to offer.   **INSIGHT 63**

Your Turn

Write about your recent experiences with salespeople. Which of these experiences do you feel were most successful? Why? Which were least successful? Why?

_____

_____

_____

THE DISCIPLINARY INTERVIEW

This interview, in many ways the most difficult of all, takes place both formally and informally in business. It ranges from the staged dressing-down of a senior manager before the CEO or board of directors to the quick, in-the-hall reprimand for an employee who takes an extended lunch break.

Purposes of the Disciplinary Interview

- To change undesirable behavior through constructive questions and discussion.
- To maintain and even increase good working relations between superior and subordinates.

Common Problems

1. *Those disciplined misunderstand criticism as a personal attack.* "Hate the sin, not the sinner," goes the old Methodist saying. Questions and assertions in a disciplinary interview must be phrased carefully so that the individual does not feel demeaned or disliked. The reason for such care is obvious: An individual can hope to change aspects of behavior but wilts at the thought of having to become an entirely different person to please the boss.

2. *The interviewer fails to hear the other side of the story.* Even in open/shut cases of policy or procedure violation, a manager should take time to ask for and listen to the disciplined person's side of the story. Often that version will contribute valuable information on how the problem can be avoided in the future.

3. *The interview concludes on a negative note.* If, in fact, the goal of the disciplinary interview is to change behavior, then the end of that interview should emphasize benefits of "doing it right" next time. The disciplined person, understanding his or her mistakes, should then be motivated to work toward positive goals. The agony of defeat, in other words, has to be accompanied by the thrill of victory.

Sample Introduction to the Disciplinary Interview

Herb, I want to talk to you about your behavior regarding coming to work on time and completing your work. What we'll discuss won't go into your file at this point and won't leave this office. But I'm deeply concerned about this situation and I've heard that others have problems with the behavior as well, given the emphasis on teamwork in this environment. I want to hear your perspective and come up with some solutions.

Sample Questions

1. Why do you think you're here for this discussion?
2. What is your side of the story?
3. Have you experienced problems such as this before? When? What were the circumstances?
4. Why do you think the problem occurred?
5. What, in your view, would have prevented this problem?
6. Why don't others you work with have this problem?
7. Are other persons or factors to blame that I should know about? Explain.
8. If you were in my position, how would you handle this situation?
9. What were the specific details of the situation as you remember them?
10. Why did the problem occur when it did and not before?
11. Are there similar problems that I should know about?
12. Who knows about this problem? How did they respond?
13. Will the problem occur again in the future? If not, how will you prevent it?
14. Are you aware of the company's usual procedures for dealing with this problem? If so, what are they?
15. Are there reasons why these procedures should not be applied to you? If so, what are those reasons?
16. What could the company or I do to prevent this problem from occurring again?
17. Do you think others are likely to have this problem? Why? What can the company or I do to help?
18. What are you willing to do to make up for this problem?
19. How do you feel about your future in this company?
20. What will you do to keep this problem from recurring?
21. In your opinion, what has been the impact of this problem on the company? On our coworkers? On your career?
22. What special circumstances should I know about before deciding what to do about this problem?
23. When did you first discover that the problem had come to light? How did you respond?
24. Were the policies and procedures of the company clearly communicated to you during your employment? If not, what did you misunderstand?
25. Are there questions about this discussion or about the problem that you would like to ask me?

INSIGHT 64	*A disciplinary interview should be viewed not primarily as an opportunity to punish but instead as a chance to clarify and motivate.*

Your Turn

Do you believe that employees respond most effectively to punishment or encouragement? Which has the greatest effect on productivity, in your opinion? Are there times when an employee must be punished instead of encouraged?

_____

_____

_____

_____

_____

_____

Summing Up

Both the persuasion/sales interview and the disciplinary interview have motivation at their core. Both forms of communication try to bring about desired action, and both have their greatest success when the "carrot" of advantages is used more than the "stick" of punishment or fear.

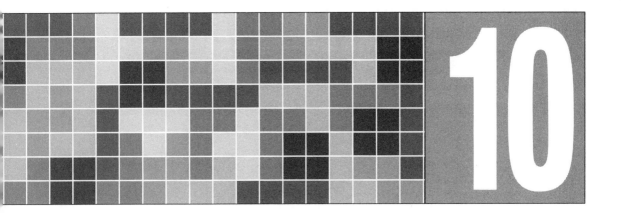

The Career-Planning Interview, Focus Group Interview, and News/Press Conference Interview

COALS

- Understand the value and techniques of the career-planning interview in aiding decision making for job fulfillment and success.

- Crasp the strategies and methods of the focus group interview in ferreting out opinion, preference, and judgment.

- Recognize techniques appropriate to the news/press conference interview.

THE CAREER-PLANNING INTERVIEW

The career-planning interview is carried out extensively on high school and college campuses as well as in business. Some interviews involve a battery of written tests designed to measure, with validated accuracy, areas of special talent and skill.

Purposes of the Career-Planning Interview

- To match a person's preferences, experience, and abilities with job tasks.
- To assist the person in making personal decisions with regard to career choices.
- To make the best possible use of company or school personnel through effective career guidance.

Common Problems

1. *The interviewee feels pigeonholed.* There is a natural tendency to label and categorize people: Joe is a computer type, Mary is a natural trainer, Frank is a born manager, and so forth. These stereotypes must be left at the door in a successful career-planning interview. Proper career choices emerge only when the spectrum of choices is as unrestricted as possible.

2. *The interviewer plays God.* On the slimmest of verbal and even non-verbal evidence, the interviewer may pronounce, "No, I don't think you're the type to pursue a career in finance." How does the interviewer know? By an untied shoelace, perhaps, indicating inattention to detail? These seat-of-the-pants judgments must be suppressed, especially when dealing with relatively impressionable young adults who trust their career counselors.

3. *The interviewee is given a plethora of choices but no basis on which to make a final decision.* Variety of choices is not necessarily freedom of choice; at times variety alone can paralyze decision making. Career interviewers should show interviewees not only what's available but also what factors they should consider in making a choice. Some of these factors are work condition, the degree to which tasks are structured, the amount and type of supervision, and the nature of and need for feedback. These form the criteria by which the interviewee can eventually come to firm personal decisions.

Sample Questions

1. What do you do well?
2. What do others say about your work?
3. What is your idea of an ideal job?

4. What do you like most about your present job? What do you like least?

5. How do you feel about the tasks you're now asked to do?

6. Describe your supervisor's management style. How does he or she direct your work? How do you feel about that form of supervision?

7. How are you most like your coworkers? How are you most unlike them?

8. What tasks are you prepared to do according to your education?

9. What tasks are you prepared to do according to your experience?

10. If your friends had to pick a proper job for you, what would it be?

11. Tell me about a recent task you worked on. How did you feel about it?

12. Describe to me where you see yourself professionally in three (five, ten) years. Give me a good idea of what you're thinking and feeling about yourself at that time.

13. Name someone you admire in the company. Why do you admire that person? In what ways would you like to be like that person?

14. Name two or three jobs you would hate to do. What do they all have in common that you dislike?

15. Tell me about your interpersonal abilities. How do you get along with people? How do people feel about you?

16. Imagine that you supervise the work of 10 other people. What problems do you think would come your way in the first year?

17. How do you think a manager should motivate people who work for him or her?

18. Name two or three jobs you might like to have. What do they all have in common?

19. What barriers get in your way as you try to accomplish your own goals in your present job? How do you deal with those barriers?

20. Do you feel appreciated for what you do now? How is that appreciation expressed? If no appreciation is expressed, how do you think it should be expressed?

21. How valuable do you think you are to the company? What would make you even more valuable?

22. What are your financial goals? Are you meeting your financial objectives for this period in your life?

23. What balance do you try to keep between work and play in your life? How well are you keeping that balance in your present job?

24. What would you like to accomplish most in your lifetime?

25. What puzzles you most about yourself?

| INSIGHT 65 | *The career-planning interview should begin without prior assumptions. What you have done in the past is no guarantee that you will find fulfillment or success by pursuing that path in the future.* |

Your Turn

Choose five of the previous questions that seem to apply most insightfully to your own career planning. Write answers for each of the five questions you choose.

_____

_____

_____

_____

_____

_____

THE FOCUS GROUP INTERVIEW

In development, survey, and marketing situations, focus groups are used more and more as an efficient way to pretest ideas and products. In effect, a cross-section of likely users (or experts in user needs) are assembled for an in-depth review of a new concept, product, or service. The feedback accumulated through this interview determines revision and development plans.

Purposes of the Focus Group Interview

- To expose a new idea, service, or product in a relatively unstructured way to a selected audience.
- To gather responses, attitudes, and insights from a target audience through questions and discussion.

Common Problems

1. *The focus group feels constrained to be extreme in its judgments.* Particularly when group members are paid for their participation (as is usually the

case), they feel pressure to "do a really good job." For some, this means adopting a hypercritical attitude; they have dozens of suggestions for improving the item at hand. For others, payment brings on an attack of niceness: The product or idea is praised to the skies. Both responses are less than useful. The sponsor of the focus group wants to know how people think and feel, not how they *think* they should think and feel.

2. *The focus group leader is sometimes dictatorial.* Some leaders develop an extensive agenda of questions, then march through them, in checklist fashion, with the group barely keeping up. Group members find themselves nodding yes or no to the leader's assertions rather than giving their own opinions.

3. *The focus is out of focus.* In contrast to the problem of dictatorship, some focus groups are left to wander through impressions without any guidance. Conversation strays to other products, industry issues, personal experiences unrelated to the product at hand, and everything except what the sponsor of the focus group wants: attitudes and responses that can be used for revision and development of the product.

Sample Questions

1. What do you see in this item that you like? Why?
2. What do you see here that you dislike? Why?
3. What aspects of this item seem especially useful?
4. To whom will this item appeal most? Why?
5. How large do you think the likely audience for this item will be?
6. What are the major competitors to this item?
7. In what ways is this item better than the competition? Worse? About the same?
8. How much would you pay for this item?
9. What would be the best way to advertise this product?
10. What should be added to (or taken away from) this item?
11. What do you associate with this item? Why?
12. How well do you like the way this item is packaged or organized?
13. What do you see as disadvantages of using this item?
14. How would you improve this item?
15. What possible uses do you see for this product?
16. What do you like about competing products?
17. What do you dislike about competing products?
18. How easy would this product be to use?
19. What difficulties would you face in using this product?
20. What should accompany this item to make a complete package?

21. How do you feel about the design of this item?
22. Would you recommend this item to friends? What would you tell them about it?
23. How long would you estimate the life expectancy of this item to be?
24. How would you introduce this item to the market?
25. What questions would you like to ask about this item?

INSIGHT 66	*Focus group interviews attempt to pierce beneath people's rational judgments to assess their subconscious and irrational feelings and attitudes toward products and services.*

Your Turn

If you have been a member of a focus group, tell how it went. What do you believe was done well? What could have been done better? If you have not been a member of a focus group, write about a topic or item you would like to explore by means of a focus group. Select several questions from the previous list that you would use in your focus group.

THE NEWS/PRESS CONFERENCE INTERVIEW

This interview is usually conducted under the pressures of time and circumstance. The interviewer may have to meet a deadline; the interviewee may have limited time at a press conference. As a result, questions must be direct and clear. The suggested questions in this section can be used at all levels of news interviewing, from politics to in-house company newsletter reporting.

Purposes of the News/Press Conference Interview

- To state questions in such a way that the interviewee must respond succinctly and candidly.
- To follow up on the implications or ambiguities of the interviewee's responses in order to draw out as definitive an answer as time will allow.

Common Problems

1. *The interviewee often controls the interviewer.* In large press conferences, such as those conducted by the president, the point of a finger from the interviewee determines who will ask questions. Often, favored reporters get called on again and again. Interviewers fight this tendency by behavior just at the edge of impertinence: They call out questions, wave arms in the air, and generally make themselves hard to ignore.

2. *Unfocused questions allow the interviewee to escape difficult or uncomfortable answers.* Questions beginning with "What do you have to say about . . . ?" and "Can you comment on . . . ?" are notoriously vague. The interviewee is usually free to respond by mentioning only the most favorable aspects of the topic at hand. By contrast, questions beginning with "Did you . . . ?" or "Is it true that . . . ?" tend to pin the interviewee down to specific answers.

3. *Poor follow-up questions let the interviewee off the hook.* When an interviewee hasn't answered the question or has tried to snow the audience with a blizzard of bureaucratic clichés, the interviewer must be ready with sharp follow-up questions that point out the inadequacy of the first response and force the interviewee to face the issue directly. Good follow-up questions often begin with "Please answer the question: Did you . . . ?" or "Let me bring you back to the question: Is it true that . . . ?"

Sample Questions

1. Is it true that . . . ?
2. Did you . . . ?
3. How do you explain the fact that . . . ?
4. How do you respond to allegations that . . . ?
5. Why did you refuse to . . . ?
6. How do you justify your decision to . . . ?
7. Who is responsible for . . . ?
8. Who should take credit (or blame) for . . . ?

9. What information can you give us about . . . ?

10. Are rumors true that . . . ?

11. Your critics claim that . . . . How do you answer them?

12. Your supporters defend you by saying . . . . Is that your defense as well?

13. What will be the impact of your decision on . . . ?

14. How will this course of action affect . . . ?

15. How will you restructure the company in order to . . . ?

16. Who will be appointed to . . . ?

17. What do you plan to do about . . . ?

18. What were you trying to accomplish when you . . . ?

19. How do you answer charges that you . . . ?

20. From whom will you pick in choosing . . . ?

21. Whom will you consult in making your decision to . . . ?

22. When can we expect a decision on . . . ?

23. What do you say to people who complain that . . . ?

24. How much will it cost the company to . . . ?

25. How many workers will be affected by . . . ?

INSIGHT 67	*Attitudes and emotions in the news/press conference interview must usually be earnest to solicit candid answers, but most stop short of overt anger or sarcasm, which will cause an interviewee to withhold information entirely.*

Your Turn

Take time to observe a press conference on television. Write about what reporters seem to do well and not so well. Next, write about what the interviewee(s) did well or not so well.

_____

_____

_____

_____

_____

_____

Summing Up

The career-planning interview offers the interviewee an opportunity to explore options, under the guidance of an interviewer trained to stimulate discussion but not to force decisions. The focus group interview is widely used throughout government, business, and academia as a way of soliciting feedback and checking perceptions. Finally, the news/press conference interview is perhaps the primary channel by which the public learns of important news from government and business sources.

More generally, interviewing in all its forms is the growth tip of a company's life—the place where new talent is discovered and hired, where obstacles are discussed and overcome, and where strategies are devised and undertaken. The ability to interview and be interviewed is a crucial career skill for getting the job you want, moving to other jobs within the company, and helping to bring aboard the brightest and best as your coworkers.

Recommended Reading

Adler, L. *Hire with Your Head.* New York: Wiley & Sons, 1998.

Bermont, T. *10 Insider Secrets to Job Hunting Success.* New York: 10 Step Corporation, 2001.

De Jong, P., and I. K. Berg. *Interviewing for Solutions.* New York: Wadsworth, 2001.

Ivey, A. E., and M. B. Ivey. *Intentional Interviewing and Counseling,* 4th ed. New York: Wadsworth, 1998.

Jones, C. *Winning with the News Media.* New York: Video Consultants, 2001.

Krueger, R. A., and M. A. Casey. *Focus Groups,* 3rd ed. New York: Sage, 2000.

Miller, W. R., and S. Rollnick. *Motivational Interviewing,* 2nd ed. New York: Guilford Press, 2002.

Still, D. J. *High Impact Hiring.* New York: Management Development Systems, 2001.

Wendleton, K. *Interviewing and Salary Negotiation.* New York: Career Press, 1999.

Year, N. M., and L. Hough. *Power Interviews.* New York: Wiley & Sons, 1998.

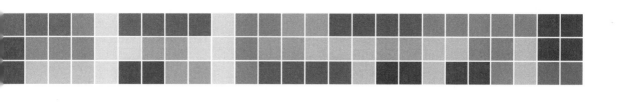

Index